Higher GCSE Mathematics
Revision and Practice

Homework Book

David Rayner

OXFORD
UNIVERSITY PRESS

Great Clarendon Street, Oxford OX2 6DP

Oxford University Press is a department of the University of Oxford.
It furthers the University's objective of excellence in research, scholarship,
and education by publishing worldwide in

Oxford New York

Auckland Cape Town Dar es Salaam Hong Kong Karachi
Kuala Lumpur Madrid Melbourne Mexico City Nairobi
New Delhi Shanghai Taipei Toronto

With offices in

Argentina Austria Brazil Chile Czech Republic France Greece
Guatemala Hungary Italy Japan South Korea Poland Portugal
Singapore Switzerland Thailand Turkey Ukraine Vietnam

Oxford is a registered trade mark of Oxford University Press
in the UK and in certain other countries

Database right Oxford University Press (maker)

First published 2006

British Library Cataloguing in Publication Data

Data available

ISBN 0 19 915138 5

ISBN 978 019 915138 7

10 9 8 7 6 5 4 3 2 1

Printed and bound in Great Britain by Bell and Bain Ltd; Glasgow

Acknowledgements

The image on the cover is reproduced courtesy of Wire Design/Digital Vision.

1   Number 1

Homework 1A

1.1 pages 1–3

1 Here are four number cards.

    a Use all the cards to make the largest possible number.
    b Use all the cards to make the largest possible **odd** number.
    c Use all the cards to make the smallest possible **even** number.

2 Write the number that is one hundred more than
    a 562
    b 914
    c 10 316·1

3 Write these numbers in figures
    a fifteen thousand, three hundred and three
    b a quarter of a million
    c six billion
    d nine hundred and nine thousand and nine.

4 Arrange each set of numbers in order of size, smallest first.
    a 6132, 6320, 6233, 6129
    b 1·7,   1·67,   1·067, 1·635
    c 0·2,   0·035, 0·155, 0·012

5 Write each statement and say whether it is true or false.
    a $0·6 = 0·60$ **b** $50p = £0·05$ **c** $£3 + 25p = £3·25$
    d $0·01 = \dfrac{1}{100}$ **e** $5·22 = 5 + \dfrac{2}{10} + \dfrac{2}{100}$ **f** $£0·4 = 4p$

6 Here are six number cards.

    Use all six cards to make the largest possible answer to each
    calculation.

    a ☐☐ + ☐☐ + ☐☐
    b ☐☐☐ − ☐☐☐

Homework 1B C

Work these out, without using a calculator.
Show your working.

1 3219 − 2183   **2** 541 − 262
3 435 × 8   **4** 3246 ÷ 6
5 45 × 11   **6** 2548 ÷ 7
7 562 + 489 − 376   **8** 26 × 200
9 725 × 8   **10** 2952 ÷ 9
11 2001 + 376 − 1850   **12** 26 × 3000

In questions **13** to **18** copy the calculations and find the missing digits.

13 a
```
    1 5 6
  + □ 2 3
  -------
    8 □ □
```
b
```
    5 6 □
  + □ 3 5
  -------
    7 □ 8
```
c
```
    □ 6 1
  + 2 6 □
  -------
    8 □ 0
```

14 a
```
    7 4 6
  + 1 □ 2
  -------
    □ 7 □
```
b
```
    3 □ 5
  + 4 4 8
  -------
    □ 9 □
```
c
```
    5 6 6
  + □ 6 □
  -------
    9 □ 1
```

15 a
```
      5 □
  ×     4
  -------
    2 2 4
```
b
```
      6 □
  ×     6
  -------
    3 9 0
```
c
```
    □ □ 6
  ×     7
  -------
  2 2 8 2
```

16 a □□□ ÷ 3 = 50

  b □□ × 4 = 112

  c 8 × □ = 72

  d □□□ ÷ 6 = 36

17 a
```
    7 □ 3
  + 1 6 □
  -------
    □ 9 0
```
b
```
    6 □ 5
  + □ 6 □
  -------
    9 2 8
```
c
```
    □ 4 □
  + 2 □ 7
  -------
    6 7 1
```

18 a □□ × 8 = 280

  b □□ × 10 = 73□

  c 56 ÷ □ = 28

  d □□□ ÷ 9 = 32

Homework 1C

1.2 pages 5–8

Work these out, without using a calculator. Show your working.

1 5·8 + 3·72   **2** 8 − 1·2   **3** 8·2 + 0.035

4 4·83 − 3   **5** 3·2 − 8·5 + 10·7   **6** 12 − 0·45

7 1·52 × 100   **8** 1·04 × 1000   **9** 16·8 ÷ 10

10 6·4 × 0·2   **11** 0·4 × 0·5   **12** $(0·3)^2$

13 Copy the diagram and fill in the missing numbers so that the answer is always 0·4.

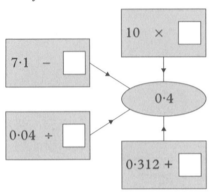

14 Find the total cost of ten magazines at £0·65 and seven CDs at £3·95 each.

15 The contents of a box weigh 1·28 kg when it is a quarter full. How much do the contents of a full box weigh?

16 Mrs Johnson buys stationery for £3·73 and pays with a £5 note. Her change consists of four coins. What are the coins?

Homework 1D

1.2 pages 9–11

Work these out, without using a calculator. Show your working.

1 45 × 27   **2** 29 × 63   **3** 207 × 36

4 5635 ÷ 23   **5** 2128 ÷ 38   **6** 33 318 ÷ 54

7 A man earns £25 608 in a year. How much does he earn each month?

8 Steve wants to be a professional squash player. He practises for 14 hours a week at a cost of £10 per hour. What is the cost of a year's practice?

9 A bear and her cub eat food weighing 676 kg in a year. How much do they eat on average each week?

10 Tins of salmon are packed 32 to a box. How many boxes are needed for 1526 tins?

11 Copy and complete.

     a ☐☐ × 43 = 11 395   **b** ☐☐☐ 5 ÷ 17 = 245

Homework 1E C

1.3 pages 14–16

1 Write all the factors of
  a 8   **b** 18   **c** 60

2 Which of these are prime numbers?
  1   2   3   4   5   23   27   39   51

3 Copy and complete the diagrams to write 104 and 396 as products of prime factors.

a
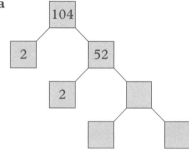

b
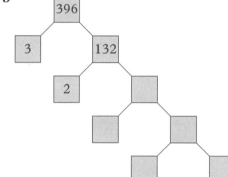

4 Look at these numbers.
  17   25   27   30   31   40
  a Which number is a factor of 100?
  b Which numbers are prime?
  c Which is a square number?
  d Which is a cube number?

5 Kevin adds some consecutive square numbers.
  This is what he writes.

  $1^2 + 2^2 + 3^2 + \ldots + n^2 = 385$

  How many square numbers did Kevin add?

6 Write a number, apart from 1, which is both a square number and a cube number.

7 a Express 1584 as the product of its prime factors.
  b Find the smallest number which can be multiplied by 1584 to give a square number.

Homework 1F**C**

1.3 pages 17–18

1 Write the first five multiples of 4.

4, 8, 12, ☐, ☐

2 Write the first five multiples of

  a 7   **b** 11

3 **a** Write the first four multiples of 8.
  b Write the first four multiples of 12.
  c Hence write the L.C.M. of 8 and 12.

> The L.C.M. is the *least common multiple.*

4 **a** Write all the factors of 45.
  b Write all the factors of 60.
  c Find the H.C.F. (highest common factor) of 45 and 60.

5 Find the H.C.F. of 24 and 60.

6 Copy the grid and use a pencil for your answers (so that you can rub out mistakes).
Write the numbers from 1 to 9, one in each box, so that all the numbers
satisfy the conditions for both the row and the column.

	Even number	Square number	Prime number
Factor of 14	2		
Multiple of 3			
Between 3 and 9			

> Remember:
> Write just **one** number in each box.

7 Copy the grid and write the numbers from 1 to 9, one in each box.

	Factor of 10	More than 3	Factor of 18
Square number			
Even number			
Prime number			

8 This one is more difficult. Write the numbers from 1 to 16, one in each box.
There are several correct solutions. Ask another student check yours.

	Prime number	Odd number	Factor of 16	Even number
Numbers less than 7				
Factor of 36				
Numbers less than 12				
Numbers between 11–17				

Homework 1G

1.4 pages 20–25

1 Copy and cancel these fractions to their simplest form.

   a $\frac{15}{24}$ **b** $\frac{21}{28}$ **c** $\frac{55}{60}$ **d** $\frac{56}{63}$

2 Find the odd one out.

   a $\frac{6}{8}, \frac{21}{28}, \frac{14}{20}, \frac{3}{4}$ **b** $\frac{24}{40}, \frac{33}{55}, \frac{6}{10}, \frac{36}{48}$

3 Here are some number cards.

   a Use two cards to make a fraction that is equal to $\frac{1}{3}$. $\frac{\square}{\square}$

   b Use three cards to make a fraction equal to $\frac{2}{9}$. $\frac{\square}{\square\square}$

   c Use three of the cards make the smallest fraction you can. $\frac{\square}{\square\square}$

4 Work out, showing your working.

   a $\frac{3}{5} + \frac{1}{4}$ **b** $\frac{5}{7} - \frac{1}{2}$ **c** $2\frac{1}{2} + \frac{2}{3}$

   d $\frac{5}{6} \times \frac{9}{10}$ **e** $1\frac{1}{2} \times \frac{4}{5}$ **f** $\frac{5}{6} \div \frac{1}{3}$

   g $6 \div \frac{3}{4}$ **h** $\frac{3}{5} \div \frac{1}{10}$

5 Copy the diagram and fill in the missing numbers so that the answer is always $\frac{2}{5}$.

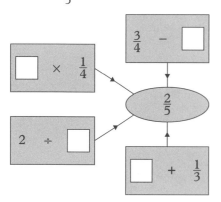

Homework 1H🄲

1.5 pages 26–29

> To estimate the answer to a calculation, round the numbers
> in the calculation, for example,
> $19 \cdot 2 \times 4 \cdot 82 \approx 20 \times 5 \approx 100$
> $724 \div 52 \cdot 7 \approx 700 \div 50 \approx 14$

Write each calculation and decide, by estimating which answer is
closest to the exact answer.

	Calculation	A	B	C
1	$2 \cdot 05 \times 9 \cdot 7$	10	30	20
2	$3 \cdot 8 \times 52 \cdot 3$	20	200	90
3	$96 \cdot 8 \times 3 \cdot 18$	35	150	300
4	$1 \cdot 03 \times 77 \cdot 5$	80	40	400
5	$46 \cdot 7 \times 98 \cdot 5$	500	2000	5000
6	$7 \cdot 94 \div 3 \cdot 91$	5	8	2
7	$69 \cdot 4 \div 8 \cdot 97$	7	3	70
8	$401 \cdot 4 \div 4 \cdot 19^2$	50	100	25
9	$10 \cdot 013 \div \sqrt{97 \cdot 4}$	0·2	1	0·1
10	$997 \div 2 \cdot 13$	500	800	2000

In questions **11** to **13** there are six calculations and six answers. Write
each calculation and decide by estimating which is the correct answer
to that calculation.

11 **a** $4 \cdot 9 \times 10 \cdot 2 =$ **b** $10 \cdot 7 \times 6 \cdot 1 =$
   c $4 \cdot 8 \times 5 \cdot 3 =$ **d** $7 \cdot 9 \times 10 \cdot 3 =$
   e $1 \cdot 1 \times 2 \cdot 7 =$ **f** $1 \cdot 8 \times 6 \cdot 4 =$
The answers are 25·44, 2·97, 81·37, 49·98, 65·27 and 11·52.

12 **a** $8 \cdot 7 \times 9 \cdot 4 =$ **b** $0 \cdot 5 \times 8 \cdot 3 =$
   c $7 \cdot 2 \times 1 \cdot 9 =$ **d** $11 \cdot 8 \times 3 \cdot 3 =$
   e $5 \cdot 2 \times 10 \cdot 8 =$ **f** $4 \cdot 3 \times 6 \cdot 8 =$
The answers are 29·24, 38·94, 81·78, 13·68, 56·16 and 4·15.

13 **a** $1 \cdot 8 \times 10 \cdot 4 =$ **b** $9 \cdot 8 \times 9 \cdot 1 =$
   c $7 \cdot 9 \times 8 \cdot 1 =$ **d** $4 \cdot 02 \times 1 \cdot 9 =$
   e $3 \cdot 8 \times 8 \cdot 2 =$ **f** $8 \cdot 15 \times 5 \cdot 92 =$
The answers are 63·99, 18·72, 31·16, 7·638, 89·18 and 48·248.

Homework 1IC

1.5 page 30

1 Round these numbers to 2 decimal places.

  a 11·731   **b** 0·8524   **c** 3·024   **d** 18·111

  e 204·655   **f** 0·671   **g** 0·083   **h** 0·984

2 Round these numbers to 2 significant figures.

  a 18·72   **b** 187   **c** 2413   **d** 0·746

  e 0·8524   **f** 60 400   **g** 111·65   **h** 245 617

3 Copy and complete this table.

Number	Rounded to 1 dp	Rounded to 1 sf	Rounded to 2 sf
0·564	0·6		
5·46			
180·52			
19·064			
0·0782			
206·55			

4 Work these out on a calculator and give the answers to 1 decimal place.

  a $11·2^2$ **b** $98·7 \div 8·35$ **c** $\sqrt{181·05}$ **d** $88·6 \times \sqrt{7}$

  e $\dfrac{12·6}{11·7} \times 8$ **f** $\dfrac{6·9}{8·1 - 3·72}$ **g** $\dfrac{8·21^3}{207}$ **h** $88·3 - \dfrac{1·9}{10·07}$

Homework 1JE

1.6 pages 31–33

1 Write these ratios in a simpler form.

  a 12 : 8   **b** 20 : 50   **c** 18 : 24   **d** 25 : 40

2 In a class there are 18 boys and 7 girls. What fraction of the class are girls?

3 Express each ratio in its simplest form. Remember to use the same units in both parts of the ratio.

  a £5 : 80p   **b** 25p : £2   **c** 600 g to 1 kg

4 Divide £75 between two people in the ratio 2 : 3.

5 A sum of £1000 is divided in the ratio 1 : 3 : 4. What is the smallest share?
Arthur, Bess and Charles share a cake weighing 450 g in the ratio
4 : 5 : 6 respectively. How heavy was Charles's share?

6 Pat and Ray share the cost of a coach trip in the ratio 3 : 1. What percentage of the cost does Ray pay?

7 Two squares are shown with their perimeters.

  a Write the ratio of the lengths of their sides.

  b Find the ratio of their areas.

perimeter = 16 cm   perimeter = 24 cm

8 On a map with scale 1 : 10 000, the distance between two points is 4 cm. Find the actual distance between the two points, giving your answer in metres.

9 Copy and complete this table.

	Map scale	Length on map	Actual length on land
a	1 : 50 000	10 cm	☐ km
b	1 : 80 000	8 cm	☐ km
c	1 : 4500	5 cm	☐ m

10 The distance between two points is 600 m. How far apart, in cm, will they be on a map of scale 1 : 1000?

11 The scale of a map is 1 : 50 000. The actual distance between two towns is 2 km. How far apart will they be, in cm, on the map?

12 The scale of a map is 1 : 1000. What area does 1 cm^2 on the map represent?

13 Find x if
   a $x : 2 = 7 : 4$ **b** $x : 3 = 12 : x$

Homework 1K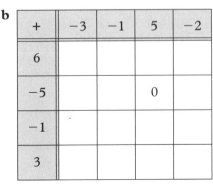

1.7 pages 35–36

1 List each set of temperatures from the coldest to the hottest.
   a $-4\,°C, 3\,°C, -8\,°C$ **b** $-5\,°C, 0\,°C, -3\,°C, 1\,°C$
   c $22\,°C, -8\,°C, -11\,°C, -2\,°C$ **d** $5\,°C, -2·5\,°C, -3\,°C, -1\,°C$

2 Copy these sequences and find the next two numbers in each.
   a $9, 7, 5, 3, —, —$ **b** $14, 10, 6, 2, —, —,$ **c** $10, 5, 0, —, —$
   d $-6, -4, -2, —, —$ **e** $-8, -7, -6, —, —$ **f** $11, 7, 3, —, —$

Work out.

3 $7 - 4$	**4** $4 - 7$	**5** $2 - 8$	**6** $3 - 11$
7 $-2 + 4$	**8** $-3 - 7$	**9** $-8 - 8$	**10** $-9 + 2$
11 $-4 + 9$	**12** $4 - 11$	**13** $-15 - 3$	**14** $-6 + 6$
15 $5 - 7 + 9$	**16** $3 - 11 + 10$	**17** $-8 - 6 + 2$	**18** $-4 + 5 - 6$
19 $2 + (-9)$	**20** $-3 - (-3)$	**21** $-4 + (-5)$	**22** $8 - (-7)$
23 $-2 + (-20)$	**24** $3 - (+5)$	**25** $-5 - (-7)$	**26** $-7 + (-4)$

27 Copy and complete these addition squares.

a

+	5	2	-3	-7
-4		-2		
0				
-3				
6				

b

+	-3	-1	5	-2
6				
-5			0	
-1				
3				

Homework 1L❻

1.7 pages 37–38

Work out.

1 $-5 \times (+2)$	**2** $-3 \times (-2)$	**3** $-8 \times (4)$	**4** $12 \div (-2)$
5 $-10 \div (-2)$	**6** $(-6)^2$	**7** $-1 \times (-1)$	**8** $8 \times (-2)$
9 $-12 \div (-6)$	**10** $16 \div (-4)$	**11** $-24 \div (4)$	**12** $49 \div (-7)$
13 $-8 \times (-7)$	**14** $-42 \div (-7)$	**15** $3 \times (-10) \times (-1)$	**16** $-4 \times (6) \times (-3)$
17 $10 \times (-60)$	**18** $3{\cdot}2 \times (-10)$	**19** $-2{\cdot}5 \div (-10)$	**20** $100 \times (-100)$

21 Copy and complete these multiplication squares.

a

×	−3	−1	5	−2	3
2					
−4			8		
1					
−5					
−1					

b

×	7	−1	0	−3	5
−5					
1					5
3					
−6				18	
10					

In questions **22** to **33** you are given

$$a = 4$$
$$b = -3$$
$$c = -1.$$

Evaluate these.

22 $a + b$	**23** $a - c$	**24** bc	**25** $a^2 + c^2$
26 ab	**27** $c - b$	**28** $a - b$	**29** $a + b + c$
30 $2a + 3b$	**31** $4cb$	**32** $8(a + b)$	**33** $a(b + c)$

Homework 1M❻ Mixed questions involving negative numbers

1.7 pages 35–38

> **Reminders**
>
> **a** $-3 - 4 = -7$ (Use a number line). **b** $6 - (-2) = 6 + 2 = 8$
>
> **c** $-5 \times -2 = 10$ **d** $8 \div (-2) = -4$

Work out.

1 $-7 + 3$	**2** -3×4	**3** $-3 - (-4)$	**4** $8 \div (-2)$
5 $-4 \times (-4)$	**6** $-8 - 5$	**7** $4 + (-2)$	**8** -3×1
9 $6 - 12$	**10** $0 \times (-7)$	**11** $-8 - 4$	**12** $-1 \times (-8)$
13 $12 \div (-3)$	**14** $10 \times (-10)$	**15** $18 - 30$	**16** $3 - (+8)$

17 $-16 \div 8$	**18** $-7 - 4$	**19** -4×5	**20** $-8 + 13$
21 $-8 + 2$	**22** $3 \times (-3)$	**23** $8 \div (-8)$	**24** $6 - (-3)$
25 $-6 \times (-1)$	**26** -3×0	**27** $-6 + 1$	**28** $-8 - 7$
29 $-30 + 42$	**30** $-2 + (-2)$	**31** $-4 - (-8)$	**32** $-100 + (-15)$

In questions **33** to **41** the box contains either $+$, $-$, $\times$ or $\div$.
Write each statement with the correct operation.
For example, $6 \,\square\, -2 = 8$ becomes $-6 \,\boxed{-}\, -2 = 8$

33 $8 \,\square\, -3 = 5$ **34** $10 \,\square\, -2 = -20$ **35** $-12 \,\square\, -2 = 6$

36 $-4 \,\square\, -2 = 8$ **37** $-12 \,\square\, -2 = -10$ **38** $8 \,\square\, -3 = 11$

39 $-100 \,\square\, -5 = 20$ **40** $-7 \,\square\, 7 = 0$ **41** $11 \,\square\, -2 = -22$

42 Copy each statement and write 'true' or 'false'.
     a $-2 > -3$ **b** $6 < (-3)^2$ **c** $6 - (-6) = 12$
     d $0 > -2$ **e** $-3 - 3 = 6$ **f** $-7 < -2$
     g $(-2)^2 = -4$ **h** $-8 + 6 + 2 = 0$ **i** $1000 \div (-10) = -100$

Homework 1N

1.8 pages 38–41

Draw **a copy** of this crossnumber pattern.
Find the answers using a calculator.
Where there are decimals put the point on the line
between the squares.

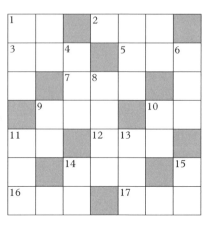

Across

1 $\sqrt{3136} \times 1{\cdot}5$

2 $\sqrt{45\,678}$ (to 3 sf)

3 $191{\cdot}1 \div 2{\cdot}6$

5 $\dfrac{131 + 67}{7}$ (to 3 sf)

7 $766 + \sqrt{4761}$

9 30% of 1170

10 $152 - \sqrt{3481}$

11 $432 - (17 \times 22)$

12 $\dfrac{27{\cdot}39}{2{\cdot}14 - 2{\cdot}074}$

14 80% of 650

16 37×3^3

17 $\dfrac{2{\cdot}63}{1{\cdot}41 \times 0{\cdot}012}$ (to 3 sf)

Down

1 $47{\cdot}2 \times 21{\cdot}5 \times 0{\cdot}86$ (to 3 sf)

4 $611 - (5{\cdot}2 \times 5)$

6 7^3

8 π (to 4 sf)

9 $\dfrac{42}{2{\cdot}4 - 1{\cdot}3}$ (to 2 sf)

10 $120 - \sqrt{625}$

11 22% of 2450

13 $\dfrac{1}{0{\cdot}0997^2}$ (to 3 sf)

14 $\dfrac{41}{7} + 0{\cdot}0015$ (to 2 sf)

15 $\dfrac{\sqrt{(169)} \times 40}{8}$

2 Number 2

Homework 2A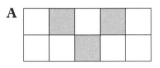

2.1 pages 46–48

1 For each diagram write
   a what fraction is shaded
   b what percentage is shaded.

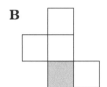
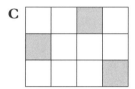

A   **B**   **C**

2 Change to percentages.
   (**Reminder** To change a fraction to a percentage, you
   multiply by 100%.)
   a $\frac{3}{5}$ **b** $\frac{1}{20}$ **c** $\frac{3}{10}$ **d** $\frac{11}{25}$ **e** $\frac{45}{60}$

3 In a test Nicki got 14 out of 20. What is her percentage mark?

4 In a survey 37 out of 40 pandas said that they preferred organic
   bamboo to bamboo grown with artificial fertilisers. What percentage
   was that?

5 In a 60-minute maths lesson, Wayne spent 18 minutes 'trying to find
   his calculator'. For what percentage of the lesson was he searching?

6 Work out these amounts.
   a 20% of £55   **b** 5% of £400   **c** 7% of £600

7 Work out these amounts, and give answers to the nearest penny.
   a 17% of £8·65   **b** 11% of £19·50   **c** 13% of £53·33
   d $8\frac{1}{2}$% of £85   **e** $6\frac{1}{2}$% of £125·80   **f** 3·7% of £120

8 Copy these and write the missing numbers as decimals.
   a 64% of 820 = ☐ × 820
   b 11% of 2550 = ☐ × 2550
   c 2% of 65·3 = ☐ × 65·3

Homework 2B

2.1 pages 49–51

1 Liz was earning £220 a week and then got a 5% pay rise. How much was she earning after the pay rise?

2 Work out the new price.
   a Increase a price of £80 by 4%.

   b Increase a price of £240 by 11%.

   c Reduce a price of £700 by 8%.

3 a Which is greater, 60% or $\frac{2}{3}$?

   b Which is greater, $\frac{3}{4}$ or 70%?

4 Abraham bought a watch for £55 and then sold it so that he made a 20% profit. At what price did he sell the watch?

5 Find the total bill

   3 brushes at £2·40 each
   4 tins of paint at £3·60 each
   VAT at 17·5% is added to the total.

6 Jackie has seen two microwaves on sale.

A		B
£ 135 including VAT	or	£ 120 plus VAT

Find the difference between the prices of the microwaves.

7 Harry invested £1400 in a bank at 4·5% interest. How much did Harry have in the bank after one year?

8 In a sale the price of a sofa was reduced by 40% and then, a month later, by a further 25%. What is the final sale price of a sofa which originally cost £950?

Homework 2C🄲

2.1 pages 51–53

> **Reminder**
>
> $$\text{Percentage increase} = \frac{\text{actual increase}}{\text{original value}} \times \frac{100}{1}\%$$

1 The price of a motor bike was increased from £2400 to £2496. Calculate the percentage increase in the price.

2 Calculate the percentage increase.

	Original price	Final price
a	£850	£901
b	£14 600	£14 892
c	£66·50	£73·15

3 The population of a village went down from 880 to 836. Calculate the percentage decrease in the population.

4 After his last film a successful actor's fee went up from £2 million to £3·25 million. What was the percentage increase in his fee?

5 Steve bought a car at an auction for £1600 and two weeks later sold it for £1824. Calculate his percentage profit.

6 Given that $M = ab$, find the percentage increase in M when both a and b are increased by 8%.

Homework 2D🄲

2.1 pages 54–55

> After an increase of 8%, the price of a boat is £7560.
> What was the price before the increase?
> 108% of old price = £7560
> 1% of old price   = £(7560 ÷ 108)
> 100% of old price = $\frac{7560}{108} \times 100$ = £7000

1 After an increase of 5%, the price of a printer is £472·50. What was the price before the increase?

2 After a 7% pay rise, the salary of Mrs Everett was £24 075. What was her salary before the pay rise?

3 After a **decrease** of 10% the price of a telephone is £58·50. Copy and complete

$$90\% \text{ of old price} = £58\cdot50$$

$$1\% \text{ of old price} = £\boxed{}$$

$$100\% \text{ of old price} = £\boxed{}$$

4 During one year the value of Mr Pert's house went down by 6%. Its value was then £60 160. What was its value before the decrease?

5 Copy the table and find the missing prices.

	Item	Old price	New price	Percentage change
a	i-Pod		£180·50	5% decrease
b	Computer		£391·60	11% decrease
c	House		£103 090	22% increase

6 The manager of a football team works for 310 days per year. Of this he spends 42 days looking at new players he might buy. What percentage of his working days is this?

Homework 2E◉

2.1 pages 55–57

> £8000 is invested at 3% compound interest.
> After 1 year, amount = 8000 × 1·03 = £8240
> After 2 years, amount = 8000 × 1·03 × 1·03 = £8487·20
> After n years, amount = $8000 \times 1·03^n$

1 A bank pays 5% compound interest per annum. Mrs Cameron puts £5000 in the bank. How much has she after
a one year
b two years?

2 Nadia invested £3000 for 3 years at 4% per annum compound interest. How much money did she have at the end of three years?

3 Tom put £3000 in a savings account offering 6% per year compound interest. How much did he have in the account after 3 years?

4 Sasha saved £4000 at 4% simple interest per year. Sylvie saved £4000 at 3·5% compound interest per year. Calculate how much each woman had in her savings account after 5 years.

5 A tennis club has 250 members. The number of members increases by 20% each year. Calculate the number of members after 3 years.

6 A tree increases in height by 12% per year. It is 20 cm tall when it is one year old.
After how many years will the tree be 5 metres tall?

Homework 2F

Use the brackets keys to work out $7{\cdot}23 - \dfrac{1{\cdot}2}{1{\cdot}53}$.

 $\boxed{7{\cdot}23}$ $\boxed{-}$ $\boxed{(}$ $\boxed{1{\cdot}2}$ $\boxed{\div}$ $\boxed{1{\cdot}53}$ $\boxed{)}$ $\boxed{=}$

The answer is $6{\cdot}446$ to 4 sf.

Work out, correct to four significant figures.

1 $85{\cdot}3 \times 21{\cdot}7$ **2** $18{\cdot}6 \div 2{\cdot}7$ **3** $10{\cdot}074 \div 8{\cdot}3$

4 $0{\cdot}112 \times 3{\cdot}74$ **5** $8 - 0{\cdot}11111$ **6** $19 + 0{\cdot}3456$

7 $0{\cdot}841 \div 17$ **8** $11{\cdot}02 \times 20{\cdot}1$ **9** $18{\cdot}3 \div 0{\cdot}751$

10 $0{\cdot}982 \times 6{\cdot}74$ **11** $\dfrac{8{\cdot}3 + 2{\cdot}94}{3{\cdot}4}$ **12** $\dfrac{6{\cdot}1 - 4{\cdot}35}{0{\cdot}76}$

13 $\dfrac{19{\cdot}7 + 21{\cdot}4}{0{\cdot}985}$ **14** $7{\cdot}3 + \left(\dfrac{8{\cdot}2}{9{\cdot}5}\right)$ **15** $\left(\dfrac{6{\cdot}04}{18{\cdot}7}\right) - 0{\cdot}214$

16 $\dfrac{2{\cdot}4 \times 0{\cdot}871}{4{\cdot}18}$ **17** $19{\cdot}3 + \left(\dfrac{2{\cdot}6}{1{\cdot}95}\right)$ **18** $6{\cdot}41 + \dfrac{9{\cdot}58}{2{\cdot}6}$

19 $\dfrac{19{\cdot}3 \times 0{\cdot}221}{0{\cdot}689}$ **20** $8{\cdot}3 + \dfrac{0{\cdot}64}{0{\cdot}325}$ **21** $2{\cdot}4 + (9{\cdot}7 \times 0{\cdot}642)$

22 $11{\cdot}2 + (9{\cdot}75 \times 1{\cdot}11)$ **23** $0{\cdot}325 + \dfrac{8{\cdot}6}{11{\cdot}2}$ **24** $8{\cdot}35^2 - 25$

25 $6{\cdot}71^2 + 0{\cdot}64$ **26** $3{\cdot}45^3 + 11{\cdot}8$ **27** $2{\cdot}93^3 - 2{\cdot}641$

28 $\dfrac{7{\cdot}2^2 - 4{\cdot}5}{8{\cdot}64}$ **29** $\dfrac{13{\cdot}9 + 2{\cdot}97^2}{4{\cdot}31}$ **30** $(3{\cdot}3 - 2{\cdot}84)^2$

31 $\dfrac{(12{\cdot}9 - 8{\cdot}45)^2}{4{\cdot}3}$ **32** $\left(\dfrac{4{\cdot}4 + 6{\cdot}23}{9{\cdot}9}\right)^2$ **33** $\dfrac{5{\cdot}89}{7 - 3{\cdot}83}$

34 $\dfrac{102}{58{\cdot}1 + 65{\cdot}32}$ **35** $\dfrac{18{\cdot}8}{3{\cdot}72 \times 1{\cdot}86}$ **36** $\dfrac{904}{65{\cdot}3 \times 2{\cdot}86}$

37 $12{\cdot}2 - \left(\dfrac{2{\cdot}6}{1{\cdot}95}\right)$ **38** $8{\cdot}047 - \left(\dfrac{6{\cdot}34}{10{\cdot}2}\right)$

39 $14{\cdot}2 - \left(\dfrac{1{\cdot}7}{2{\cdot}4}\right)$ **40** $\dfrac{9{\cdot}75 - 8{\cdot}792}{4{\cdot}31 - 3{\cdot}014}$

In questions **41** to **48** use the key for the fractions.

41 $\dfrac{3}{7} + \dfrac{1}{3}$ **42** $\dfrac{2}{5} \times \dfrac{3}{14}$ **43** $\dfrac{5}{9} - \dfrac{1}{2}$ **44** $1\dfrac{2}{3} + \dfrac{8}{9}$

45 $2\dfrac{1}{4} \div 1\dfrac{1}{2}$ **46** $31 \div \dfrac{5}{7}$ **47** $5\dfrac{3}{4} \times 2\dfrac{1}{2}$ **48** $\left(1\dfrac{1}{4}\right)^2 - \dfrac{9}{16}$

Homework 2G C

2.3 pages 65–67

$$4500 = 4 \cdot 5 \times 1000 = 4 \cdot 5 \times 10^3 \qquad 0 \cdot 00042 = 4 \cdot 2 \times 10^{-4}$$
$$640 = 6 \cdot 2 \times 10^2 \qquad\qquad\qquad 0 \cdot 005 = 5 \times 10^{-3}$$

A Rewrite these numbers in standard form.

1 3200	**2** 18 000	**3** 4300	**4** 580
5 700 000	**6** 2600	**7** 48	**8** 27 000
9 650 000	**10** 30 000	**11** 2 500 000	**12** 800
13 13	**14** 2000	**15** 624 000	**16** 20 million
17 0·026	**18** 0·007	**19** 0·000 012	**20** 0·000 352
21 0·000 001 67	**22** 0·0009	**23** 0·002 58	**24** 0·434
25 0·0211	**26** 0·000 000 805		

B Write these standard form numbers as ordinary numbers.

1 $2 \cdot 4 \times 10^2$	**2** $3 \cdot 6 \times 10^3$	**3** $1 \cdot 9 \times 10^4$	**4** $8 \cdot 3 \times 10^3$
5 $7 \cdot 5 \times 10^2$	**6** $4 \cdot 8 \times 10^5$	**7** $9 \cdot 2 \times 10^3$	**8** $6 \cdot 3 \times 10^1$
9 $7 \cdot 2 \times 10^4$	**10** $2 \cdot 6 \times 10^5$	**11** 7×10^{-2}	**12** 8×10^{-1}
13 2×10^{-5}	**14** $4 \cdot 7 \times 10^{-4}$	**15** $2 \cdot 13 \times 10^{-2}$	**16** $1 \cdot 72 \times 10^{-3}$

C Work out these and give your answers in standard form.

1 $(4 \times 10^3) + (5 \times 10^5)$ **2** $(6 \times 10^2) + (2 \times 10^3)$ **3** $(8 \times 10^4) + (2 \times 10^6)$
4 $(2 \times 10^{-2}) + (7 \times 10^{-3})$ **5** $(8 \times 10^{-1}) + (3 \times 10^{-3})$ **6** $(5 \times 10^2) + (1 \times 10^{-1})$

Homework 2H C

2.3 pages 68–69

$$(2 \times 10^4) \times (3 \times 10^5) = (2 \times 3) \times 10^{4+5} = 6 \times 10^9$$
$$(8 \times 10^5) \times (2 \times 10^{-3}) = (8 \times 2) \times 10^{5-3} = 16 \times 10^2 = 1 \cdot 6 \times 10^3$$
$$(9 \times 10^8) \div (3 \times 10^2) = (9 \div 3) \times 10^{8-2} = 3 \times 10^6$$

Work out these and write your answers in standard form.

1 $(3 \times 10^2) \times (2 \times 10^1)$	**2** $(4 \times 10^3) \times (2 \times 10^1)$
3 $(4 \times 10^1) \times (1 \times 10^6)$	**4** $(8 \times 10^3) \times (2 \times 10^4)$
5 $(7 \times 10^2) \times (4 \times 10^{-3})$	**6** $(5 \times 10^3) \times (7 \times 10^{-1})$
7 $(6 \times 10^2) \times (6 \times 10^{-1})$	**8** $(4 \times 10^{-2}) \times (3 \times 10^{-1})$
9 $(8 \times 10^7) \div (2 \times 10^3)$	**10** $(7 \times 10^5) \div (1 \times 10^2)$
11 $(6 \times 10^2) \div (3 \times 10^{-1})$	**12** $(7 \times 10^2) \div (5 \times 10^{-1})$

13 a To work out $(1.75 \times 10^2) \times (3 \times 10^9)$, using a calculator, press these keys.

| 1·75 | EXP | 2 | × | 3 | EXP | 9 | = |

The answer is 5.25×10^{11}.

b To work out $(8 \times 10^4) \div (2 \times 10^{-3})$, press these keys.

| 8 | EXP | 4 | ÷ | 2 | EXP | − | 3 | = |

What is the answer?

Work out these and write your answers in standard form.

14 $(7.2 \times 10^2) \times (3 \times 10^1)$ **15** $(3.5 \times 10^2) \times (7 \times 10^4)$

16 $(6.7 \times 10^5) \times (4 \times 10^7)$ **17** $(2.9 \times 10^2) \times (2 \times 10^1)$

18 $(4.8 \times 10^{-1}) \times (8 \times 10^6)$ **19** $(1.75 \times 10^3) \div (5 \times 10^1)$

20 $(3.72 \times 10^2) \div (6 \times 10^2)$ **21** $(1.72 \times 10^2) \div (4 \times 10^{-1})$

22 $(1.3 \times 10^4) \div (2 \times 10^2)$ **23** $(2.45 \times 10^2) \div (5 \times 10^{-1})$

24 Given that $x = 4 \times 10^7$ and $y = 3 \times 10^4$, work out

    a xy **b** $\dfrac{y}{x}$ **c** x^2

25 A pile of 20 000 sheets of paper is 1·6 metres high. Work out the thickness of one sheet of paper, in metres, and write your answer in standard form.

Homework 2I 🅒

2.4 pages 70–72

1 Find the value of each expression.

    a $4n + 11$ when $n = 15$ **b** $2(n - 7)$ when $n = 7$

    c $2n^2$ when $n = 3$ **d** $\dfrac{n}{4} + 8$ when $n = 36$

2 Find the value of the expressions given that $a = 3$, $b = 5$ and $c = -1$.

    a $4a + b$ **b** ab **c** $2c$ **d** $b + c$

    e $2(b - a)$ **f** $5(a + c)$ **g** $\dfrac{b}{10} + a$ **h** $\dfrac{a + b}{4}$

    i $a - c$ **j** abc **k** $b^2 + c$ **l** $bc + ab$

3 a Find an expression for the perimeter of this rectangle.

    b Find the perimeter when $p = 3$ and $q = 5$.

4 Given that $x = 3$ and $y = -4$, find the value of each of these expressions.

   a $2x^2 + y$ **b** $4x^2 - y$ **c** $4x - y^2$

   d $2x + 2y$ **e** $6x^2 - 4$ **f** $2y^2 + x^2$

5 Given that $a = 1$ and $d = -2$, find the value of each of these expressions.

   a $2a^2 + 4d$ **b** $3a^2 - 2d^2$ **c** $7a^2 + 5d^2$

   d $6d - 3a^2$ **e** $10d^2 - 4$ **f** $3d^2 + 4d$

6 Evaluate these expressions when $n = 2$.

   a $n(n - 2)$ **b** $3n - 1 - n$ **c** $n - 3\frac{1}{2}$ **d** $n + n^2$

   e $\dfrac{20}{n + 3}$ **f** $n(n + 3)$ **g** $\dfrac{4}{n} + \dfrac{n}{4}$ **h** $3n - 100$

Homework 2J©

2.4 pages 72–73

1 Given that $c = -4$, find the value of each of these expressions.

   a $2c^2 + 7$ **b** $2c^2 - c$ **c** $3c^2 + 3c$

   d $5c - c^2$ **e** $5c^2 + 20$ **f** $10c^2 - 1$

2 Given that $m = 6$ and $x = -1$, find the value of each of these expressions.

   a $2x^2 + m$ **b** $5m - 3x$ **c** $4m + 6x$

   d $2m^2 - 4x$ **e** $m^2 + x^2$ **f** $3x^2 - 2m$

3 Given that $c = 5$ and $t = -10$, find value of each of these expressions.

   a $2t^2 + 10c$ **b** $4c^2 + 10t$ **c** $3c^2 + 11$

   d $19 - 6c$ **e** $2c + 4t$ **f** $9c + 3t^2$

4 The perimeter of this rectangle is given
by the expression
$P = 2(a + b)$.
   a Find P when $a = 5$ cm and $b = 3·5$ cm.
   b Find P when $a = 6·3$ cm and $b = 3·7$ cm.

5 A formula connecting velocities with acceleration and time is
   $V = u + at$
Find the value of V when $u = 25$, $a = -2$ and $t = 400$.

6 Evaluate these, given that $a = 2$
                            $b = -1$
                            $c = 3$.

   a $a(c - b)$ **b** $2a(b + c)$ **c** $b^2(a + 5)$ **d** $(c - b)^2$

   e $\dfrac{ab}{c}$ **f** $\dfrac{ac + b}{b^2}$ **g** $\dfrac{2a + 3b}{2c}$ **h** $a^3 + b^3$

Homework 2K ⓒ

2.4 pages 72–73

Draw this crossnumber pattern. Complete the puzzle given that the letters have these values:

$p = -5$ $q = -10$ $r = -7$ $s = -1$ $t = 6$ $u = 4$ $w = 3$

Across

1 $pq + t$
2 $qtp + pq + r$
3 $pqu + u^2$
5 $p + pq + pqu$
7 $q^2 + qsw + w$
9 $s + q^2rs + w$
10 w^4
11 $qr + 2u$
12 $2q^2 + wt + r$
14 $q^2 - s$
16 $(qw)^2$
17 $q^2 - p$

Down

1 $pq^2s + swr$
4 $tq^2 - q$
6 $q^2ps + squ - s$
8 $q^3sw + q^2w - 2uqs$
9 $3ut + 2w$
10 $r^2 + pr - w$
11 $q^2rs + wsq + s$
13 $q^2 - q - s$
14 qs
15 $rq - p$

Homework 2L ⓒ

2.5 pages 75–78

> **Reminder**
>
> Distance = Speed × Time   Speed = $\dfrac{\text{Distance}}{\text{Time}}$ Time = $\dfrac{\text{Distance}}{\text{Speed}}$
>
> Density $= \dfrac{\text{Mass}}{\text{Volume}}$

1 Find the time taken for each journey.
   a 360 km at a speed of 20 km/h
   b 180 miles at a speed of 45 mph
   c 200 m at a speed of 5 m/s

2 A ski lift moves at a steady speed of 2 m/s. How far will a carriage go in one minute?

3 A train covers a distance of 310 miles in 5 hours. What is the average speed of the train?

4 Convert a speed of 30 metres/second into km/h.

5 Light travels at a speed of 300 000 000 m/s. Light from the sun takes 3 minutes to reach a planet. How far is the planet from the sun?

6 The density of lead is about 20 000 kg per m³.
  a Calculate the volume of this lead cylinder in cm³.
  b Convert the volume into m³.
  c Work out the mass of the cylinder, giving your answer to the nearest kg.

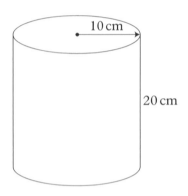

7 Silver has a density of 120 000 kg/m³. What is the volume of 9600 kg of silver?

8 The distance from Hatfield to York is 180 miles. I leave Hatfield at 7:20 a.m. and arrive at York at 10:00 a.m. What is my average speed?

Homework 2M⊙

2.6 pages 79–81

If the height of a glass is 13 cm, correct to the nearest centimetre, the actual height could be from 12·5 cm to 13·5 cm.

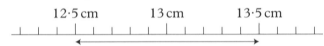

1 Meera's handspan is 18 cm, to the nearest centimetre. What is her greatest possible handspan?

2 The diameter of a saucepan is 20 cm, correct to the nearest cm. What is the least possible diameter of the saucepan?

3 The length of a car journey is 13 km, to the nearest km. What is the greatest possible length of the journey?

4 The diagram shows a weighing scale.
  a Which letter is at $4\frac{1}{2}$ kg?

  b A cake weighs at 2·5 kg, correct to the nearest 0·1 kg. What is the greatest possible weight of the cake?

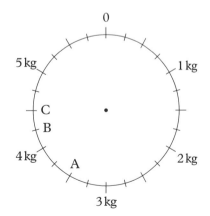

5 Copy and complete the table for each measurement.

Measurement	Lower limit	Upper limit
a Steve's height = 162 cm, to nearest cm		162·5 cm
b Steve's weight = 53 kg, to nearest kg		
c Length of envelope = 21·6 cm, to nearest 0·1 cm		
d Volume of a glass = 0·8 litres, to nearest 0·1 litre		
e Length of field = 260 m, to nearest 10 m		

6 The mass of a butterfly is 3·14 g, correct to the nearest 0·01 grams. What are the greatest and least possible masses of the butterfly?

Homework 2N Ⓔ

2.6 pages 81–83

1 The dimensions of the rectangle are measured to the nearest cm. Work out the maximum possible area of the rectangle.

5 cm

8 cm

2 The height of a shoe box is 18 cm, to the nearest cm. What is the maximum possible height of a pile of 10 boxes?

3 A rectangular pool has dimensions 11 m by 7 m, measured to the nearest metre.
   a Work out the minimum possible area of the surface of the pool.
   b What is the maximum perimeter of the pool?

4 The dimensions of a box are 12 cm × 9 cm × 5 cm, all to the nearest cm.
   Calculate the limits of accuracy for the volume of the box.

5 The sides and the angle in this triangle are given to the nearest unit. Calculate the minimum possible area of the triangle.

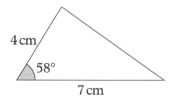

4 cm

58°

7 cm

6 You are given $m = 14·6$ and $n = 8·3$, both correct to 1 decimal place. Find the largest possible value of
   a $m + n$ **b** $m - n$

7 The area of a square is 90 cm^2, to the nearest cm^2. Work out the possible values for the side length of the square.

3   Algebra 1

Homework 3A◯

3.1 pages 92–94

1 Work through the flow diagrams and write the expressions you obtain.

a n → +5 → ×3 → ?   **b** n → ×2 → −3 → ×5 → ?

c n → ×2 → −8 → square   **d** n → ×3 → +1 → ÷7 → ?

2 Draw each diagram and fill in the missing details.

a n → ? → $n+5$ → ? → $3(n+5)$ **b** n → ? → $n-2$ → ? → $n+7$ → ? → $n+6$

c n → ? → $6n$ → ? → $6n+1$ → ? → $2(6n+1)$ **d** n → ? → $n+3$ → ? → $n-1$ → ? → $(n-1)^3$

Collect like terms together.

3 $5n + 6n$ **4** $3x - 2x + 4x$ **5** $7m + 2m - 3m$

6 $8c - 2c + c$ **7** $2m + n + 3m + 6n$ **8** $4n + 1 + 5n + 10$

9 $6a + 10 - 2a - 2$ **10** $6h - 2y + 2h - 9y$ **11** $8y - 3 + y + 9$

12 $4x - 10 - 2x + 3$ **13** $x^2 + 12y + 3x - 2y$ **14** $7y + 5 + 7y - 4 + y^2$

15 $3a - 2c + 5c - 2a$ **16** $5x + 2y - 7y + 5x$ **17** $7d - 4c + 10 - 6d + 4c$

Copy and complete.

18 $3n + \square + 2 = 8n + 2$

19 $5m + \square + 2n + \square = 6m + 10n$

20 $8a + \square + \square + 3b + 11 = 10a + 10b + 11$

21 $x^2 + 2x + \square + 3x + \square = x^2 + 8x + 7$

22 $x^2 + 8x + \square + 9x + \square = x^2 + 20x + 1$

23 Find the perimeter of each quadrilateral. Give the answers in their simplest form.

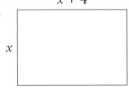

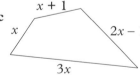

a rectangle: top $x+4$, side x

b rectangle: top x, side $2x$

c quadrilateral: $x+1$, $2x-1$, x, $3x$

24 Write in a simpler form (for example, $4m \times 3n = 12mn$).

   a $6a \times 2b$ **b** $4n \times 3p$ **c** $5n \times 6m$ **d** $a \times 3n$ **e** $p \times 6q$

   f $n \times 2n$ **g** $3n \times 4n$ **h** $6n \times 3n$ **i** $7a \times 7a$

Homework 3B C

3.1 pages 94–97

Remove the brackets from these expressions.

1 $2(x + 3)$ **2** $5(b - 4)$ **3** $8(a - 2)$ **4** $3(x + c)$
5 $7(t - y)$ **6** $10(m + 1)$ **7** $6(y + 2)$ **8** $4(u - x)$
9 $n(n + 2)$ **10** $n(n - 3)$ **11** $n(n - 10)$ **12** $x(2x + 1)$
13 $x(3x - 2)$ **14** $x(4x + 1)$ **15** $2x(3x + 1)$ **16** $2x(x - 3)$

17 Find the missing lengths in these rectangles.

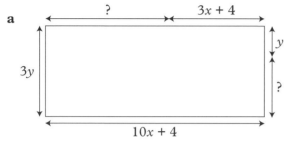
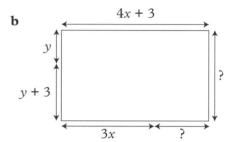

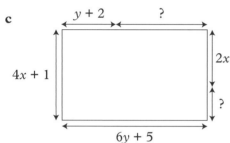
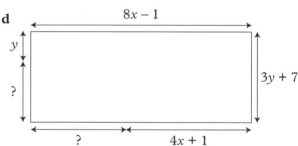

Remove the brackets and simplify.

18 $2(4x + 3) + 4(3x - 4)$ **19** $n(n + 1) + 4n$
20 $3(4d + 1) - 2(6d - 5)$ **21** $a(2a - 1) + a^2$
22 $5a + 2(3a + 4) - 2a$ **23** $x(x + 2) - x(x - 1)$
24 $9y - 5(y + 2) - 3$ **25** $2a(a - 3) + a(3a - 1)$
26 $11b + 3 - 3(2b - 5)$ **27** $n(1 - 2n) + 3n(1 + n)$

28 Here are some algebra cards.

| $x + x + x$ | $x^2 + x$ | $x + 2$ | $4x - x$ |

| $2x + 2$ | $2x$ | $x^2 + 2x - x$ | $2x + 1$ |

a Which two cards will always give the same answer as $\boxed{3 \times x}$?

b Which two cards will always give the same answer as $\boxed{x(x + 1)}$?

c Which card will always give the same answer as $\boxed{2(x + 1)}$?

Homework 3C ⓒ

3.1 pages 94–97

1 Find three pairs of equivalent expressions or terms.

A $3n \times 4n$ **B** $7 \times n \times n$ **C** $4n^2$

D $7n^2$ **E** $(2n)^2$ **F** $12n^2$

In questions **2** to **13** copy the statements and answer 'true' or 'false'.

2 $7 \times n = n \times 7$ **3** $n + n = 2n$ **4** $a + a^2 = a^3$

5 $a \times a = a^2$ **6** $3m + 3m = 6m^2$ **7** $3 \times p \times q = 3pq$

8 $(3m)^2 = 9m^2$ **9** $t \times t = 2t$ **10** $a \div b = b \div a$

11 $n(n - 7) = n - 7n$ **12** $5n - n = 5$ **13** $x(x + 7) = x^2 + 7x$

14 A rough formula for changing the temperature in degrees Fahrenheit from the temperature in degrees Celsius is $F = 2C + 32$.

  a Find F when $C = 10$.

  b Find F when $C = -15$.

  c Find the temperature in degrees Celsius when it is $44\,°F$.

In questions **15** to **23** simplify the expressions.

15 $\dfrac{6a}{a}$ **16** $3(x + 1) - 4$ **17** $\dfrac{n \times n}{n}$

18 $a^2 + a^2 + a^2$ **19** $10e \div e$ **20** $3x(x + 1) - 3x$

21 $\dfrac{x + x + x}{x}$ **22** $\dfrac{4n}{4n}$ **23** $a(a + a)$

Remove the brackets and simplify these expressions.

24 $(n + 2)(n + 4)$ **25** $(n + 3)(n - 1)$ **26** $(n + 5)(n - 5)$

27 $(n - 7)(n + 3)$ **28** $(2n + 1)(n - 4)$ **29** $(3n - 4)(2n + 3)$

30 $(n + 2)^2$ **31** $(n + 1)^2 + (n - 1)^2$ **32** $2(n + 3)^2$

33 **a** Find an expression for the perimeter of the picture.

    b Find an expression for the area of the picture.

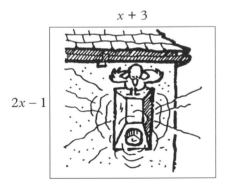

$x + 3$

$2x - 1$

Homework 3D ⊙

3.1 and 3.2 pages 99–102

In questions **1** to **6** copy and complete the statement.

1 $8a + 4b = 4(2a + \square)$

2 $5a + 15b = 5(\square + 3b)$

3 $15a + 20b = 5(\square + \square)$

4 $7a + 21b = \square (a + 3b)$

5 $27a - 36b = 9(\square - \square)$

6 $4a + 8b + 4c = 4(\square + \square + \square)$

Factorise these expressions.

7 $20x + 12y$

8 $30x - 12y$

9 $27x + 9y$

10 $35x - 14y$

11 $40x + 20y$

12 $10x + 5y + 10z$

13 $3x^2 + 2x$

14 $4x^2 + 2x$

15 $5x^2 + x$

16 $x^2 - 2x$

17 $2y^2 + 5y$

18 $12x^2 + 21x$

19 Solve these equations.

  a $n - 5 = 16$ **b** $6n + 2 = 14$ **c** $18 + n = 9$

  d $8 = n + 1$ **e** $13 = n - 5$ **f** $n + n = 10$

20 The diagrams show two equilateral triangles.
Find x and y.

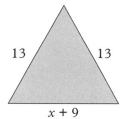
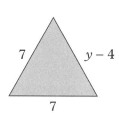

Solve these equations.

21 $3x + 7 = 13$

22 $5x + 3 = 28$

23 $3x - 2 = 19$

24 $2x - 1 = 9$

25 $4x + 3 = 4$

26 $5x + 2 = 4$

27 $9x + 8 = 35$

28 $3x - 42 = 10$

29 $6x - 1 = 0$

30 $4 + 2x = 16$

31 $0 = 3x - 66$

32 $2x + 5 = 1$

33 Find m and n in these rectangles.

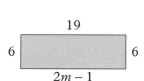
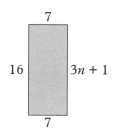

34 Find the number I am thinking of.
'If I multiply the number by 3 and then add 5, the answer is 1.'

Homework 3E ●

3.2 page 103

Solve these equations.

1 $3(x + 3) = 30$ **2** $4(x - 5) = 2$ **3** $7(2 + x) = 35$

4 $3(x + 4) = 2(x + 5)$ **5** $7(x + 2) = 4(x + 6)$ **6** $3(x - 2) = 2(x + 3)$

7 $7(x - 2) = 3x - 6$ **8** $2x + 3(x - 3) = x + 3$ **9** $3(2x - 1) - 2(x + 1) = -1$

10 Find x and y in this square.

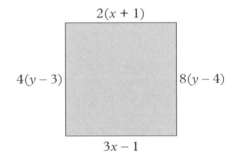

$2(x + 1)$

$4(y - 3)$ $8(y - 4)$

$3x - 1$

11 Here are four expressions involving an unknown number n.

A $3n + 1$ B $2(n + 2)$ C $n - 7$ D $2n + 1$

  a Find the value of n if the expressions A and B are equal.
  b Find the value of n if the expressions B and C are equal.
  c Which two expressions could never be equal for any value of n?

12 Find x if the perimeter of this rectangle is 12 cm.

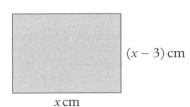

$(x - 3)$ cm

x cm

Homework 3F ●

3.2 page 104

Solve these equations.

1 $\frac{4}{x} = 2$ **2** $\frac{20}{x} = 5$ **3** $\frac{9}{x} = 2$ **4** $\frac{8}{x} - 2 = 14$

5 $\frac{x}{7} = 2$ **6** $7 + \frac{x}{9} = 11$ **7** $\frac{x}{100} = -2$ **8** $\frac{3x}{2} = 21$

9 $\frac{5}{x} = \frac{1}{2}$ **10** $\frac{3}{x} = \frac{1}{4}$ **11** $\frac{7}{x} = \frac{3}{4}$ **12** $\frac{x}{2} + 1 = 9$

13 The area of the picture is 45 cm². Find the value of x.

5 cm

$3(2x + 1)$ cm

14 Solve these equations.

   a $x^2 = (x + 2)(x - 1)$

   b $x^2 - 1 = (x + 1)(x - 3) + 8$

   c $(x + 3)^2 = x(x + 1) - 1$

15 Answer 'true' or 'false'.

   a $3x - 1 = 7$ is an equation.

   b $x^2 - 1 = (x + 1)(x - 1)$ is true for all values of x.

   c $x^2 = 4$ has only one solution.

   d $4x - 5$ is an expression.

Homework 3G **C**

3.3 pages 110–114

1 To find $\sqrt{91 \cdot 5}$ by trial and improvement you need to solve the equation $x^2 = 91 \cdot 5$.

Copy and complete these steps and give your answer correct to 1 dp.

Try $x = 9$	$9 \times 9 = $ _____	$x = 9$ is too small
Try $x = 10$	$10 \times 10 = $ _____	$x = 10$ is too big
Try $x = 9 \cdot 5$	____ $\times$ ____ $=$ _____	$x = 9 \cdot 5$ is too____
Try $x = 9 \cdot 6$	____ $\times$ ____ $=$ _____	$x = 9 \cdot 6$ is too____

$x = 9.$__ to 1 dp.

2 Use the method in question **1** to find

   a the cube root of 50, correct to 1 dp

   b the cube root of 210, correct to 1 dp.

3 This rectangle has width h cm. The length is 2 cm more than the width. The area of the rectangle is 404 cm^2.

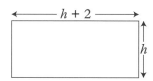

Find the value of h correct to one decimal place.

You need to solve the equation

   $h(h + 2) = 404$

Copy and complete these steps.

Try $h = 17$	$17 \times 19 = 323$	$h = 17$ is too small
Try $h = 23$	$23 \times 25 = 575$	$h = 23$ is too big
Try		

4 Find solutions to these equations, correct to one decimal place.

   a $x(x - 2) = 10$

   b $x(x + 1) = 32$

   c $3^x = 30$

Homework 3H Ⓒ

3.4 pages 115–119

> For the sequence 3 6 9 12, the nth term is $3n$.
> For the sequence 3 5 7 9, the nth term is $2n + 1$.

1 Select the correct formula for the nth term of each sequence.

 a 4, 8, 12, 16, . . .
 b 5, 10, 15, 20, . . .
 c 10, 20, 30, 40, . . .
 d 7, 14, 21, 28, . . .
 e 6, 11, 16, 21, . . .
 f 12, 22, 32, 42,

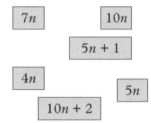

$7n$ $10n$ $5n + 1$ $4n$ $5n$ $10n + 2$

2 The first five terms of a sequence are

 4   7   10   13   16

 Copy and complete the sentence 'The nth term of the sequence is $3n + \Box$.'

3 Find the nth term of each sequence.

 a 4, 6, 8, 10, 12, . . .
 b 4, 9, 14, 19, 24, . . .
 c 11, 20, 29, 38, 47, . . .

4 Pattern 1   Pattern 2   Pattern 3

 a Draw Pattern 4.
 b Copy and complete this table.

Pattern number	1	2	3	4	5
Number of dots	1	5	9		

 c How many dots are needed for Pattern 20?
 d Find an expression for the number of dots in pattern number n.

5 The nth term of a sequence is $6n - 3$.
 Find the 5th term of the sequence.

6 The nth term of a sequence is $40 - 3n$.
 Find the 7th term of the sequence.

Homework 3I(E)

3.4 pages 119–124

1 Here is a pattern of U-shapes.

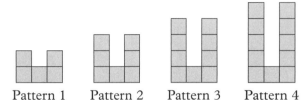

Pattern 1   Pattern 2   Pattern 3   Pattern 4

   a How many squares are needed for Pattern 6?
   b How many square are needed for Pattern n?

2 Find the nth term of each sequence.
   a 5, 8, 11, 14, ...
   b 11, 17, 23, 29, ...
   c 1, 9, 17, 25, ...

3 The diagrams show polygons with diagonals drawn from one vertex.

$n = 4$ sides $n = 5$ sides $n = 6$ sides
$d = 1$ diagonal $d = 2$ diagonals $d = 3$ diagonals

   Find a formula connecting d and n. Write '$d = $ —'.

4 Look at this pattern.   Copy and complete.
   $3^2 - 2^2 = 2 \times 3 - 1$ **a** $6^2 - 5^2 =$ ——
   $4^2 - 3^2 = 2 \times 4 - 1$ **b** $15^2 - \square =$ ——
   $5^2 - 4^2 = 2 \times 5 - 1$ **c** $n^2 - \square =$ ——

5 The nth term of a sequence is
   $$(2n)^2 + 3$$
   a Find the first term.
   b Find the fifth term.

6 Here is a sequence of squares and dots.

 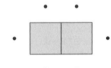 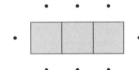

  a How many dots will surround the diagram that has a row of 20
    squares?
  b How many squares are in the diagram that has 148 dots?
  c How many dots will surround the diagram that has a row of n
    squares?

7 Use differences to help you find the nth term of these quadratic
  sequences.
  a 2, 5, 10, 17, 26, ...   **b** 9, 18, 33, 54, 81, ...
  c 2, 6, 12, 20, 30, ...   **d** 5, 14, 27, 44, ...

Homework 3JⒺ

3.5 pages 127–131

The line $y = 2x + 1$ has gradient 2 and y-intercept 1.

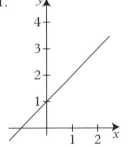

1 Find the gradients of AB, BC and AC.

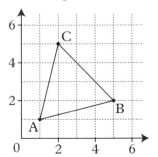

2 Find the gradients of DE, EF and FD.

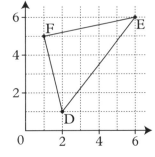

Write the equations of these lines.

3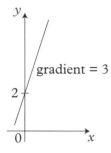

4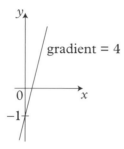

5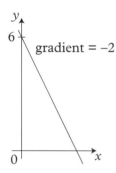

6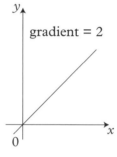

7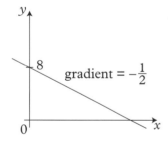

8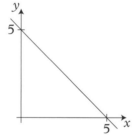

9 Find the gradient of the straight line through
   a $(2, 9)$ and $(4, 15)$
   b $(1, -1)$ and $(3, 9)$.

10 (More difficult) Find the equation of the line which passes through the points $(0, 3)$ and $(2, 7)$.

11 a Find the equation of the line that is parallel to the line $y = 3x - 11$ and which passes through the point $(0, 5)$.
   b Find the equation of the line which is perpendicular to the line $y = 2x + 5$ and which passes through the origin.

Homework 3K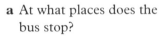

3.6 pages 133–136

1 This graph shows a bus journey from York to Skipton and back again.

   a At what places does the bus stop?

   b How long does the bus stop at Skipton?

   c At what speed does the bus travel
      i from York to Harrogate
      ii from Harrogate to Skipton
      iii from Skipton back to Harrogate?

   d When does the bus return to York?

   e When does the bus arrive at Skipton?

   f When does the bus leave Harrogate?

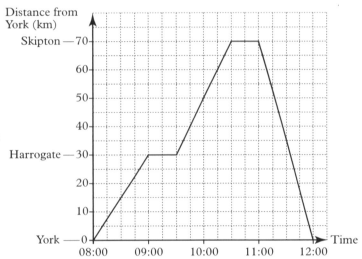

2 This graph shows a car journey from Leeds to Scunthorpe and back again.

   a For how long does the car stop at
      i Thorne
      ii Scunthorpe
      iii Selby?

   b When does the car leave
      i Thorne   **ii** Scunthorpe?

   c At what speed does the car travel
      i from Leeds to Throne
      ii from Thorne to Scunthorpe
      iii from Scunthorpe to Selby
      iv from Selby to Leeds?

   d At what time on the outward journey is the car exactly mid-way between Thorne and Scunthorpe?

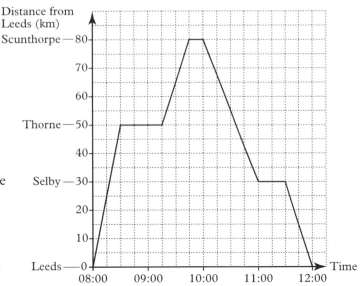

Homework 3L ⓒ

3.7 pages 139–140

1 The graph shows the lines $x + y = 11$, $4x + y = 17$ and $x - 2y = 2$.

Use the graph to solve these simultaneous equations.

a $x + y = 11$
$x - 2y = 2$

b $4x + y = 17$
$x + y = 11$

c $x - 2y = 2$
$4x + y = 17$

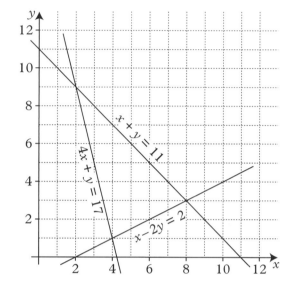

2 a Draw the graphs of $x + 2y = 8$ and $x - y = 2$.
Draw axes with x and y from 0 to 8.

b Use your graphs to solve these simultaneous equations.
$x + 2y = 8$
$x - y = 2$

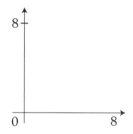

3 Solve these simultaneous equations.

a $7x + 3y = 23$
$x + y = 5$

b $4x + 7y = 26$
$4x + 3y = 18$

c $3x + 2y = 0$
$2x - y = 7$

d $2x + 5y = 16$
$4x - 3y = -7$

Homework 3M Ⓔ

3.7 pages 146–147

1 Find the coordinates of the points A and B
by solving these simultaneous equations.
$$y = x^2 + 1$$
$$y = 2x + 4$$

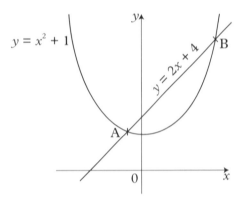

2 Solve these simultaneous equations.

a $y = 3x - 2$
$x^2 + 2y = 12$

b $y = x + 2$
$x^2 + y^2 = 100$

c $3x^2 + 2y^2 = 30$
$y + 2x = 1$

4 Shape, space and measures 1

Homework 4A ⊙

4.1 pages 151–158

Find the angles marked with letters.

1

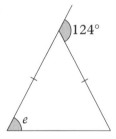

2

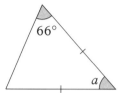

3

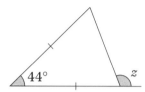

4

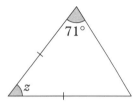

5

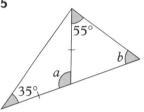

6

7

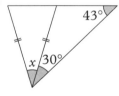

8

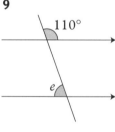

9

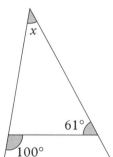

10

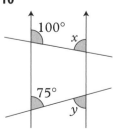

11

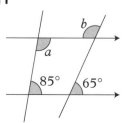

12

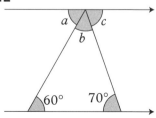

13

14

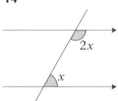

15

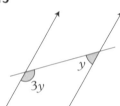

16

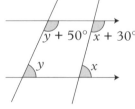

17

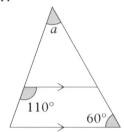

18

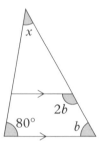

19

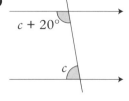

20

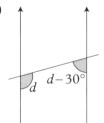

21

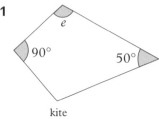

kite

22

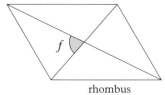

rhombus

23

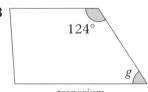

trapezium

Homework 4B

4.1 pages 159–161

1 The diagram shows a regular hexagon
with its exterior angles marked.
Calculate the size of each exterior angle.

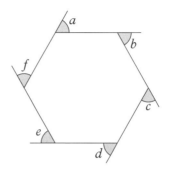

> The sum of the
> exterior angles of
> any polygon is
> 360°.

2 Find the angles x and y in this pentagon.

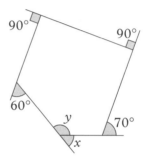

3 The diagram shows part of a regular polygon.
How many sides does the polygon have?

4 The diagram shows a regular polygon P with two
regular hexagons and a square. Find the angle a.

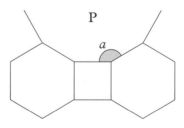

5 The diagram shows squares and equilateral
triangles joined together. Find the angle b.

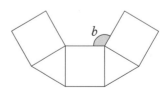

6 Work out the size of the interior angles of a regular polygon with
   a 20 sides   **b** 45 sides

Homework 4C **C**

4.3 pages 162–167

Use only a pencil, a straight edge and a pair of compasses.

1 Draw a line PQ of length 7 cm. **Construct** the perpendicular bisector of PQ.

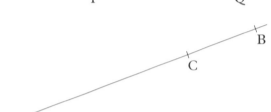

2 Draw a line AB and **construct** the perpendicular to the line segment AB which passes through the point C.

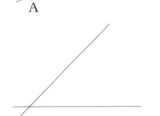

3 Draw two lines at an angle of about 45°. Construct the bisector of the angle.

4 Make a list of the pairs of shapes which are congruent.

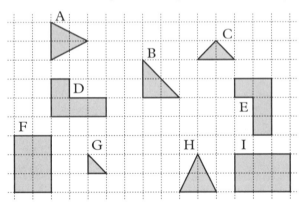

5 Which shapes in the diagram in question **4** are **similar** but **not** congruent?

6 a Copy each shape on to square grid paper and draw all lines of symmetry.
   b For each shape state the order of rotational symmetry.

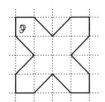 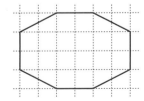 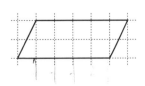

Homework 4D ❻

4.3 pages 168–171

You need a pencil, a ruler and a pair of compasses.

1 Draw two points A and B that are 8 cm apart.
Draw the locus of points which are equidistant from A and B.

A   8 cm   B

2 a Draw triangle PQR on square grid paper.
  b Construct the locus of points which are
    equidistant from lines PQ and PR.
  c Construct the perpendicular bisector of PR.

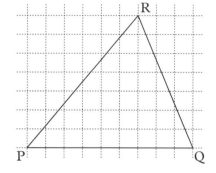

3 Triangle ABC is a scale drawing of a garden in
which 1 square = 1 m². Copy the diagram on to
square grid paper.
  a Construct the bisector of angle B.
  b Mike puts a post in the garden. He wants the
    post to be nearer to line AB than to line BC.
    He also wants the post to be within 5 m of C.

Shade the region where the post can be.

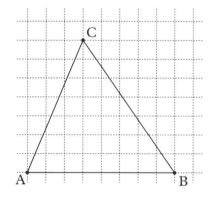

4 The diagram shows the walls of a shed,
in which 1 square = 1 m².
A dog is attached by a rope, 5 m long,
to the point P on the wall.

Draw the diagram on square grid paper
and shade the region that the dog can reach.

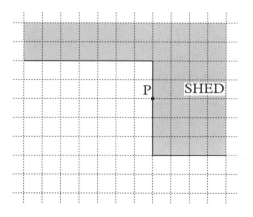

Homework 4E C

4.4 pages 171–178

Find the sides marked with letters. All lengths are in cm.
Give answers correct to 3 sf.

1
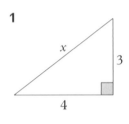

2
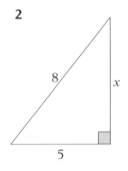

3
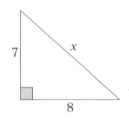

4
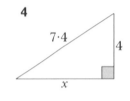

5 A rectangle of length 10 cm has diagonals of length 12 cm.
Calculate the width of the rectangle.

6 In the diagram PQ = 2·35 cm, PR = 9·5 cm and
RS = 4·1 cm. Calculate the length of QS.

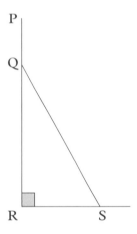

7 Calculate the length x.

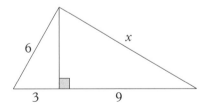

8 Calculate the length y.

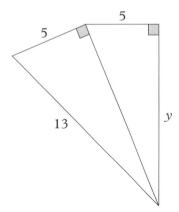

9 a Draw an equilateral triangle of side 8 cm and draw a
line of symmetry.
  b Calculate the height of the triangle.
  c Calculate the area of the triangle.

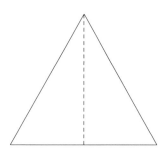

10 The diagram shows a cuboid with lengths in cm.
  Calculate **a** AC
       b AG

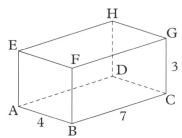

Homework 4F🇨

4.6 pages 180–188

Find the area of each shape. All lengths are in cm.

1
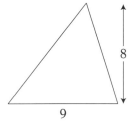

2
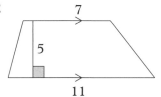

3
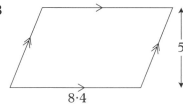

4
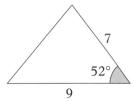

5
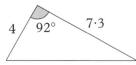

6
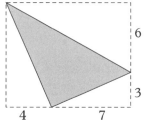

7 Find the length x. The area is shown inside the shape.

a
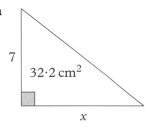

b
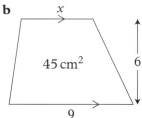

c
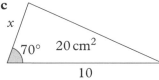

8 The area of an equilateral triangle is 85 cm². Find the length of each side of the triangle.

9 The diagram shows an isosceles triangle, in which AB = BC, joined to a square BCDE. The area of the combined shape is 100 cm². Find the length BC.

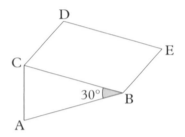

Homework 4G Ⓒ

4.7 pages 189–195

1 Find the circumference of each circle, giving your answers correct to 3 significant figures.

a
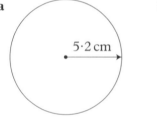
5·2 cm

b
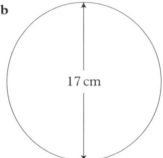
17 cm

c
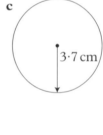
3·7 cm

2 Calculate the area of each circle in question **1**.

3 A garden is made up of a rectangle and a semicircle. Calculate the total area of the garden.

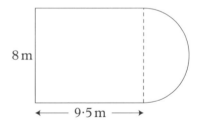

8 m

9·5 m

4 The diameter of the wheels of a car is 65 cm. The car is driven in a straight line and the wheels make 1000 complete revolutions. How far, in km, has the car moved?

Homework 4H ●

4.7 pages 189–195

1 Calculate the perimeter of each shape, which is either a semicircle or a quarter circle.

a
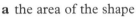
8·5 cm

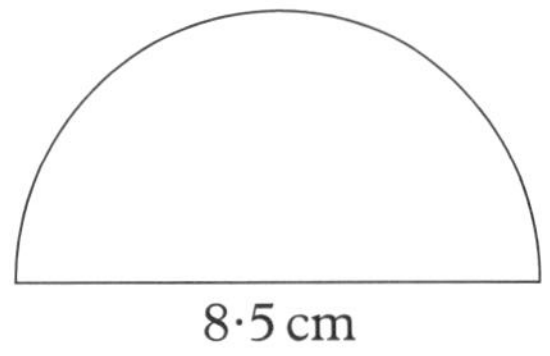

b
6·2 cm
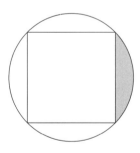

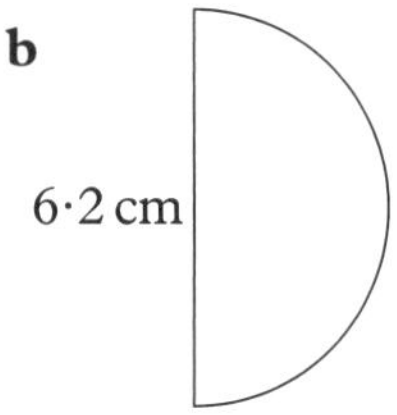

c
4·1 cm

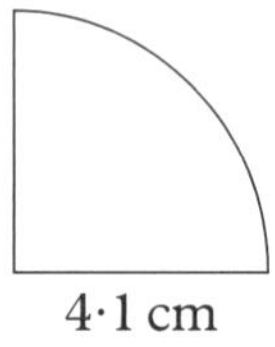

2 This shape consists of a rectangle of length 12 cm between two quarter circles of radius 5 cm. Calculate
a the area of the shape
b the perimeter of the shape.

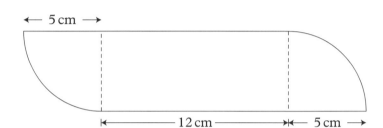

← 5 cm →

|← 12 cm →|← 5 cm →

3 Calculate the radius of a circle of circumference 65 cm.

4 Calculate the radius of a circle of area 42 cm².

5 A square is inscribed in a circle of radius 10 cm. Find the shaded area.

6 The perimeter of a semicircle of diameter d is 70 cm. Find d.

d

Homework 4I ❻

4.7 pages 198–205

1 Find the length of the minor arc AB in each circle. All lengths are in cm.

a

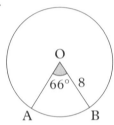

b

c

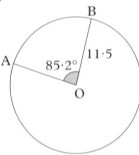

2 Calculate the area of the minor sector AOB in each diagram in question **1**.

3 The sector in the diagram has an area
of 32 cm². Work out the angle x, correct
to one decimal place.

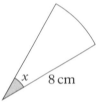

4 In the diagram OA = 6·5 cm and OB = 9 cm.
Find the shaded area.

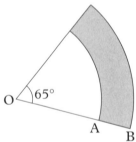

5 This circle has a radius of 10 cm.
The chord AB subtends an angle of 82°
at the centre of the circle. Calculate the
area of the minor segment, which is shaded.

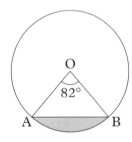

6 In the diagram OC = OD = 8 cm
and CD = 12 cm. Find the shaded area.

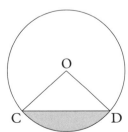

Homework 4J⦿

4.8 pages 208–212

Find the volume of each prism. All the angles are right angles and the dimensions are in centimetres.

1

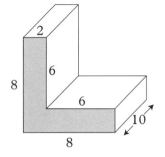

2

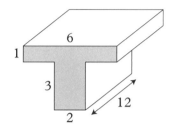

Find the volume of each cylinder, to the nearest cm³.

3

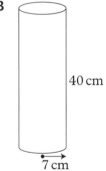

40 cm

7 cm

4

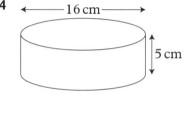

16 cm

5 cm

5 Which of the wooden rods in the diagram is heavier, if they are made of the same sort of wood?

A

2 cm

60 cm

B

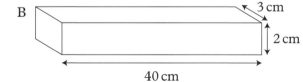

3 cm

2 cm

40 cm

6 How many times could you fill the
cylindrical glass from the large drum,
which is full of wine?

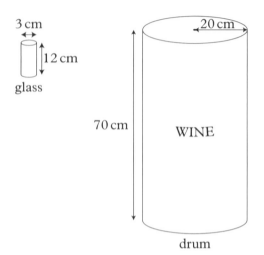

3 cm

12 cm

glass

70 cm

20 cm

WINE

drum

7 A cylindrical disc of radius 80 cm and thickness 1 cm is cut into eight
identical pieces. Calculate the volume of one of the pieces. Make a
drawing to show what one of the pieces would look like.

8 A water trough is in the shape of a half cylinder of radius 22 cm and
length 3 m. Water is poured into the trough at a rate of 200 cm^3
per second. How long will it take to fill the trough?

Homework 4K❸

4.8 pages 208–212

1 Calculate the height, h, of a cylinder of
volume 400 cm^3 and
base radius 6 cm.

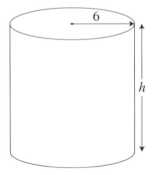

6

h

2 Calculate the radius of a cylinder of volume 850 cm^3 and height 12 cm.

3 Two coins of radius 1·8 cm and thickness
0·4 cm are melted down and recast into
a solid cube. Find the length of the side
of the cube.

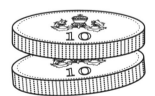

4 A solid cube of side 9 cm is melted down and recast into a solid cylinder
of height 1·6 cm. Find the radius of the cylinder.

5 A cylindrical can of internal radius
15 cm contains water to a depth
of 25 cm. A stone of volume 500 cm^3
is immersed in the water. Calculate
the rise, d, in the level of the
water in the can.

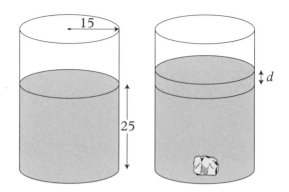

6 A cylinder of capacity 2 litres has its radius equal to
its height. Calculate the radius of the cylinder.

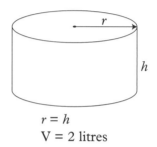

$r = h$
V = 2 litres

Homework 4L ⊙

4.8 pages 212–215

Important formulae	Sphere $V = \frac{4}{3}\pi r^3$
	Cone $V = \frac{1}{3}\pi r^2 h$
	Pyramid $V = \frac{1}{3}$(base area) × height

Find the volume of each of these solids. Give the answers correct to 3 sf.

1 **2** **3**

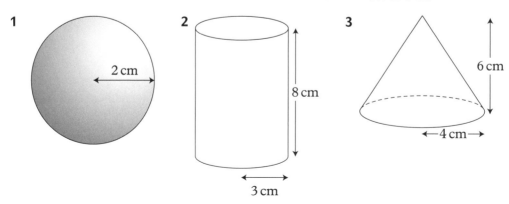

2 cm

8 cm

3 cm

6 cm

←4 cm→

4

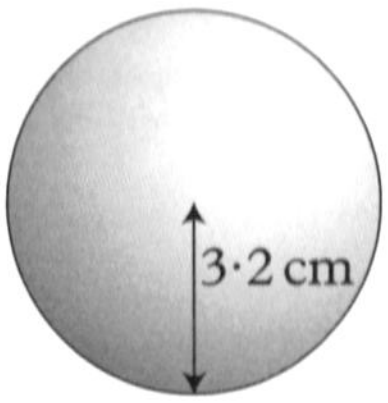

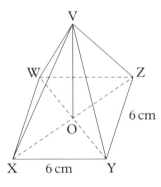

3·2 cm

5

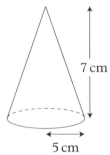

7 cm

5 cm

6

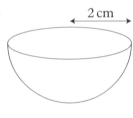

2 cm

7

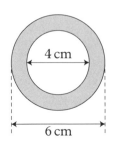

V

W   Z

6 cm

O

X   6 cm   Y

WX = XY = YZ = WZ
        = 6 cm
VO = 5 cm

8

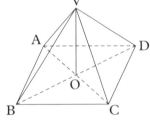

V

A   D

O

B   C

AB = DC = 3 cm
BC = AD = 6 cm
VO = 5 cm

9 The diagram shows a cross-section through the
centre of a hollow spherical ball made of steel.

4 cm

6 cm

Calculate
a the volume of steel used to make the ball
b the weight of the ball if the density of steel is 8 g/cm^3.

Homework 4M(E)

4.8 pages 212–215

1 These objects consist of a cylinder joined to a hemisphere or a cone. Find the volume of each object, correct to 3 sf.

a

b
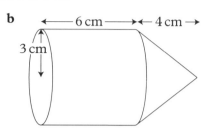

2 A solid sphere of radius 2 cm is melted down and recast into a number of discs of radius 1 cm and thickness 0·2 cm. Calculate
a the volume of the sphere
b the volume of one disc
c the number of complete discs which can be made from the sphere.

3 Liquid is poured into an inverted cone of internal radius 10 cm and height 15 cm at a rate of 6 cm^3/s. How long will it take to fill the cone?

4 Calculate the radius of each sphere.

a
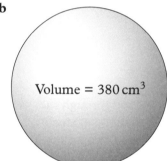
Volume
= 80 cm^3

b
Volume = 380 cm^3

5 The volume of a cone is 780 cm^3. The radius of its base is 8 cm. Calculate the height of the cone.

6 Two solid spheres of radius 6 cm are melted down and made into a single sphere. Calculate the radius of the new sphere.

7 This hemisphere has the same volume as a cylinder of height 10 cm and diameter 8 cm. Calculate the radius of the hemisphere.

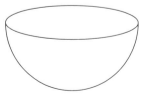
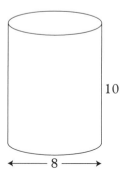
10

8

Homework 4N©

4.8 pages 217–220

> **Important formulae**
>
> **Sphere**
> Surface area $= 4\pi r^2$
>
> **Cone**
> Curved surface area $= \pi rl$,
> where l is the slant height
>
>
>
> **Cylinder**
> curved surface area $= 2\pi rh$

1 Calculate the **curved** surface area of each cylinder. All lengths are in cm.

a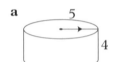
5
4

b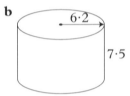
6·2
7·5

2 Calculate the **total** surface area of a solid cylinder of radius 4 cm and height 8·4 cm.

3 Calculate the **curved** surface area of each object.

a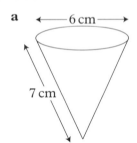
6 cm
7 cm

b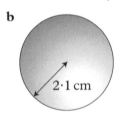
2·1 cm

c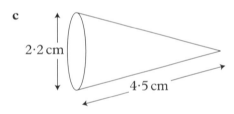
2·2 cm
4·5 cm

4 The diagram shows a solid hemisphere. Calculate the total surface area.

1·4 cm

5 Calculate the curved surface area of the cone. Notice that you are given the **vertical** height of the cone.

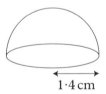
7
$r = 4$ cm
vertical height $= 7$ cm

6 Calculate the radius of a sphere which has a surface area of 900 cm^2.

Homework 40 ⊙

4.9 pages 220–224

1 Use the letters to identify pairs of similar shapes.

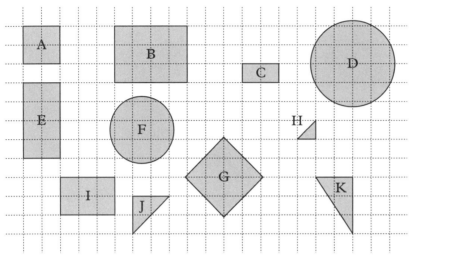

In questions **2** to **6** each pair of shapes is similar. Find the sides marked with letters. All lengths are in cm.

2

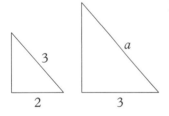

3

4

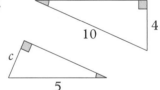

5

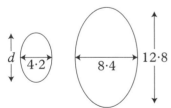

6

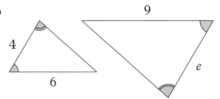

7 In a photo of a house, the front door is 1 cm high and the roof is 7 cm high. The real door is 2 m high. Find the height of the real roof.

8 a Explain why triangle ABE is similar to triangle CDE.
   b Find the length DE.

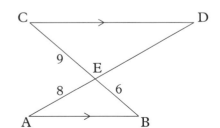

Homework 4P ⒞

4.9 pages 227–231

Here are several pairs of similar shapes. Find the areas of
shapes A, B, C and D.

1

A

Area
$8\,\text{cm}^2$

5 cm

10 cm

2

Area
$12\,\text{cm}^2$

5 cm

B

15 cm

3

10 cm

C

15 cm

Area $= 16\,\text{cm}^2$

4

D

4·2 cm

Area
$220\,\text{cm}^2$

8·4 cm

5 A piece of string of length 12 cm encloses an area of 20 cm^2.
A string of length 42 cm encloses a similar shape.
Calculate the area of the similar shape.

6 Two circles have areas 100 cm^2 and 625 cm^2. If the radius of the
smaller circle is R cm, find the radius of the larger circle, in terms of R.

7 Here are pairs of similar shapes. Find the lengths a, b, c and d.

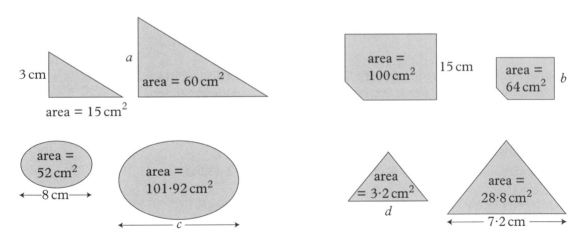

3 cm

a

area $= 15\,\text{cm}^2$

area $= 60\,\text{cm}^2$

area =
$100\,\text{cm}^2$

15 cm

area =
$64\,\text{cm}^2$

b

area =
$52\,\text{cm}^2$

8 cm

area =
$101\cdot92\,\text{cm}^2$

c

area
$= 3\cdot2\,\text{cm}^2$

d

area =
$28\cdot8\,\text{cm}^2$

7·2 cm

Homework 4Qⓔ

4.9 pages 232–235

In questions **1** to **4** each pair of shapes is similar. Find the volumes and lengths marked with letters.

1

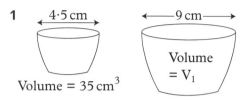

4·5 cm

Volume = 35 cm^3

9 cm

Volume = V$_1$

2

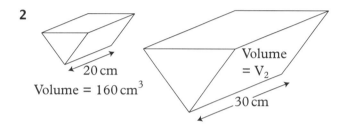

20 cm

Volume = 160 cm^3

Volume = V$_2$

30 cm

3

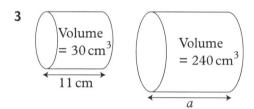

Volume = 30 cm^3

11 cm

Volume = 240 cm^3

a

4

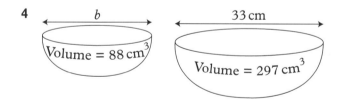

b

Volume = 88 cm^3

33 cm

Volume = 297 cm^3

5 Two similar cans have heights of 8 cm and 12 cm respectively. If the volume of the smaller can is 600 cm^3, find the volume of the larger can.

6 Two similar pyramids have volumes of 80 cm^3 and 3430 cm^3 respectively. The height of the smaller pyramid is 6 cm.
   Calculate the height of the larger pyramid.

7 'Regular' and 'Giant' bars of chocolate weigh 250 g and 432 g respectively and are similar in shape.
   a If the regular bar is 14 cm long, find the length of the giant bar.
   b The surface area of the regular bar is 100 cm^2. Find the surface area of the giant bar.

5   Algebra 2

Homework 5A 🄲

5.1 pages 241–244

Part A

Make a the subject.

1 $2a + 1 = 10$

2 $3a - 2 = 19$

3 $na + b = t$

4 $ma + v = q$

5 $pa - A = B$

6 $na - q = A$

7 $ka - w = n^2$

8 $ma + m = n$

9 $at + m = e$

10 $aB - w^2 = v^2$

11 $L + pa = d$

12 $M = ma - n$

13 $x = xa + y$

14 $v^2 = xa - t$

15 $sa - s^2 = z^2$

16 $pq + ra = x^2$

17 $lm + ab = h^2$

18 $t + ae = d + b$

19 $p^2 = m + n + Ba$

20 $km = ma - n^2$

21 $m(a - n) = t$

22 $u(a + x) = x$

23 $p(a + w) = y$

24 $A(a - u) = q$

25 $L(x + a) = m$

26 $n(x^2 + a) = x^3$

27 $r(a - r) = s^2$

28 $x(a - x) = y^2$

29 $3(a - 4) = 1$

30 $5(a + 2) = 8$

31 $T = n(a - t)$

32 $V = w(a - y)$

33 $w + q = m(a - w)$

34 $x^2 - y^2 = z(a - z)$

35 $ut + at = v^2$

36 $MN + ma = L^2$

37 $z(x + a) = x$

38 $y^2 = w(a - w)$

39 $q(a - q) = x^2 + q^2$

40 $k(m + a) = km + n$

Part B

Make k the subject.

1 $\dfrac{k}{n} = a$

2 $\dfrac{k}{t} = A$

3 $\dfrac{k}{x} = x$

4 $z = \dfrac{k}{P}$

5 $v = \dfrac{k}{w}$

6 $\dfrac{k}{n} = n^2$

7 $\dfrac{k}{m} = -e$

8 $\dfrac{k}{t} = (a - b)$

9 $\dfrac{k}{h} = x + y$

10 $\dfrac{k}{m} = -m$

11 $\dfrac{k}{(a + b)} = z$

12 $\dfrac{k}{m - n} = B$

13 $a = \dfrac{e}{k}$

14 $t = \dfrac{c^2}{k}$

15 $ab = \dfrac{e}{k}$

16 $\dfrac{h}{k} = m$

17 $\dfrac{a^2}{k} = g$

18 $\dfrac{a + b}{k} = c$

19 $\dfrac{d + e}{k} = u$

20 $\dfrac{h - a^2}{k} = \dfrac{1}{c}$

Homework 5B⊖

5.1 pages 243–245

Make n the subject.

1 $t - n = b$

2 $h - n = k$

3 $p - n = v$

4 $h - an = c$

5 $g - tn = q$

6 $h - n = h^2$

7 $a(b - n) = h$

8 $t(t - n) = d$

9 $p - nt = s$

10 $\dfrac{a}{n} + b = c$

11 $\dfrac{d}{n} - e = f$

12 $\dfrac{h}{n} + t = v$

Make x the subject.

13 $ax^2 = h$

14 $mx^2 = t$

15 $x^2 - h = m$

16 $x^2 + h = 2h$

17 $ax^2 + b = c$

18 $ax^2 + p = v$

19 $\sqrt{x - a} = c$

20 $\sqrt{a + x} = e$

21 $\sqrt{mx} = v$

22 $\sqrt{\dfrac{h}{x}} = p$

23 $\sqrt{\dfrac{m}{x}} = y$

24 $\sqrt{mx^2 - c} = d$

Make t the subject.

25 $at = b - t$

26 $nt = h + t$

27 $vt + a = t$

28 $a - vt = b - wt$

29 $\dfrac{a + t}{a - t} = 2$

30 $h(a - t) = c(a + t)$

Homework 5C⊖

5.1 pages 241–246

Make x the subject.

1 $a + x = p$

2 $y + x = m$

3 $z = k + x$

4 $u^2 = t^2 + x$

5 $a = bc + mx$

6 $z = k + ax$

7 $u^2 = e^2 + kx$

8 $m(a + x) = b$

9 $h = k(a + x)$

10 $y = p(p + x)$

11 $\dfrac{x}{k} = y$

12 $\dfrac{x}{m} = n$

13 $q = \dfrac{x}{q}$

14 $mn = \dfrac{x}{n}$

15 $\dfrac{m}{x} = a$

16 $e = \dfrac{n}{x}$

17 $w = \dfrac{u}{x}$

18 $\sin 32° = \dfrac{e}{x}$

19 $\dfrac{1}{2}zx = y$

20 $\dfrac{1}{3}kx = p$

21 $x^2 - n = m$

22 $v + x^2 = a - b$

23 $bx^2 - n = n^2$

24 $a(x - b) = d + e$

25 $k(x^2 - k) = mp$

26 $y - x = m$

27 $e(x - d) = u$

28 $a(y + x) = z$

29 $y(ex - f) = w$

30 $t(m + ax) = m$

31 $\dfrac{x}{(c + d)} = y$

32 $\dfrac{(a - b)}{x} = p$

33 $\dfrac{(m + n)}{x} = A$

34 $\dfrac{k}{x^2} = h$

35 $\dfrac{(A + B)}{x} = E$

36 $\dfrac{1}{4}kx = q$

37 $a(x^2 - d) = h$

38 $y = k^2 - x$

39 $g = m - nx$

Make *a* the subject.

40 $\sqrt{b} + a = e$

41 $\dfrac{\sqrt{a}}{f} = c$

42 $\sqrt{ab + c} = h$

43 $ha - c = d - a$

44 $ma + d = a + 2d$

45 $ca - f = h - ca$

46 The surface area of a sphere is given by the formula
$S = 4\pi r^2$
Make *r* the subject of the formula.

47 The volume of a cylinder is given by the formula
$V = \pi r^2 h$
Make *r* the subject of the formula.

48 The volume *V* of a sphere of radius *r* is given by the formula
$V = \dfrac{4}{3}\pi r^3$
Make *r* the subject of the formula.

Homework 5D ⊙

5.2 pages 247–251

a This diagram shows the inequality $x > 3$
(the circle at 3 is not filled in).

b This diagram shows the inequality $-2 < x \leqslant 2$
(the circle at 2 is filled in).

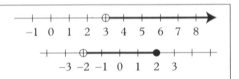

1 Write the inequalities shown in the diagrams, using the variable *n*.

a
$$-5\ -4\ -3\ -2\ -1\ 0\ 1\ 2\ 3\ 4\ 5$$

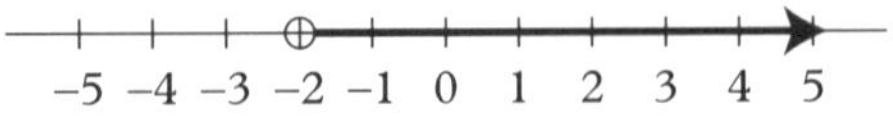

b
$$-5\ -4\ -3\ -2\ -1\ 0\ 1\ 2\ 3\ 4\ 5$$

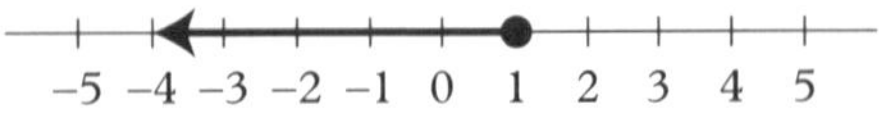

c
$$-5\ -4\ -3\ -2\ -1\ 0\ 1\ 2\ 3\ 4\ 5$$

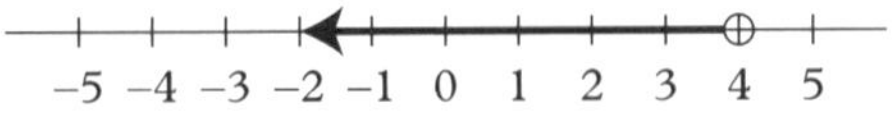

d
$$-5\ -4\ -3\ -2\ -1\ 0\ 1\ 2\ 3\ 4\ 5$$

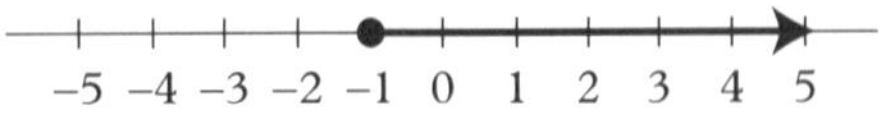

e
$$-5\ -4\ -3\ -2\ -1\ 0\ 1\ 2\ 3\ 4\ 5$$

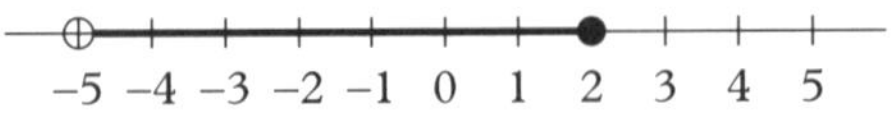

f
$$-5\ -4\ -3\ -2\ -1\ 0\ 1\ 2\ 3\ 4\ 5$$

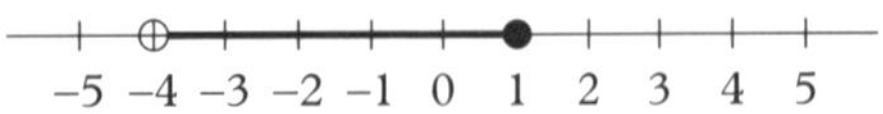

g
$$-5\ -4\ -3\ -2\ -1\ 0\ 1\ 2\ 3\ 4\ 5$$

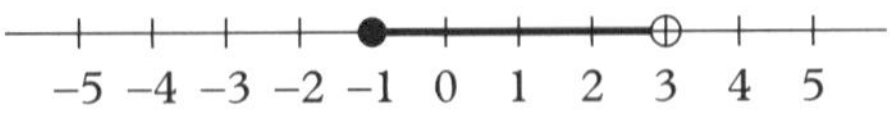

h
$$-5\ -4\ -3\ -2\ -1\ 0\ 1\ 2\ 3\ 4\ 5$$

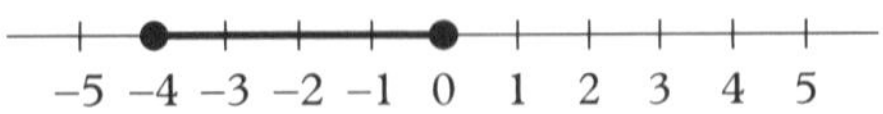

2 Show these inequalities on a number line.

a $x > 2$

b $x < -1$

c $x \geqslant -1$

d $x \leqslant 1$

e $0 \leqslant x < 4$

f $-2 < x < 2$

3 List all the whole number (or 'integer') solutions for these inequalities.

a $1 < x < 5$

b $0 < x \leqslant 5$

c $-2 \leqslant x < 2$

4 Solve these inequalities.

a $2x + 1 > 9$

b $5x - 1 < 16$

c $7x - 3 > 25$

d $\dfrac{5x - 1}{2} > 7$

e $\dfrac{2x + 1}{5} \geqslant 1$

f $3(x - 2) < 6$

5 Solve this inequality
$$8 < x - 3 < 21$$

> Solve the two inequalities separately.

6 Solve these inequalities.

a $-1 < 2x + 1 < 9$ **b** $-2 < 3x - 1 < 1$ **c** $\frac{1}{3} \leqslant \frac{x - 2}{3} \leqslant 1$

d $x^2 < 36$ **e** $x^2 > 25$

Homework 5E **C**

`5.2 pages 252–254`

Describe the shaded region in each diagram, using one or more inequalities.

1
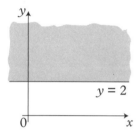

2
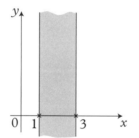

3
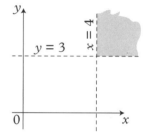

4
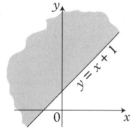

5
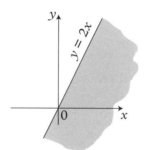

6
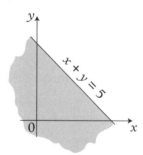

7
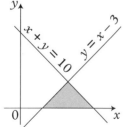

8
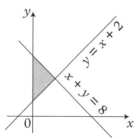

9
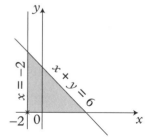

For question **10** to **15** draw a sketch graph similar to those above and indicate the set of points which satisfy the inequalities by shading the region they are in.

10 $1 \leqslant y \leqslant 4$ **11** $0 < x < 7$ **12** $y \geqslant 2, x \geqslant 0$

13 $x + y \leqslant 4$ **14** $y \geqslant x + 2$ **15** $y \leqslant 2x - 3$

Homework 5F🄲

5.3 pages 255–261

1 y is proportional to z so that $y = kz$, where k is a constant.
   Given that $y = 35$ when $z = 7$, find
   a the value of y when $z = 10$
   b the value of y when $z = 3$.

2 A is directly proportional to d^2. If $A = 12$ when $d = 2$, find
   a the value of A when $d = 1$
   b the value of A when $d = 4$.

3 Given that $y \propto x$, copy and complete the table.

x	2	3		22
y	8		40	

4 Given that $P \propto u^2$, copy and complete the table.

u	1	2		$\frac{1}{2}$
P	4		64	

5 The cost, C, of a carpet is proportional to its area, A.
   a Write a relationship between C and A and a constant k.

   A carpet of area $12\ \text{m}^2$ costs £240.
   b How much is a carpet of area $19\ \text{m}^2$?
   c What is the area of a carpet which costs £500?

Homework 5G🄲

5.3 pages 258–259

1 C is inversely proportional to p.
   a Write a relationship between C and p and a constant k.
   b Given that $C = 2$ when $p = 12$, find the value of C when $p = 3$.

2 T is inversely proportional to z. If $T = 18$ when $z = 2$, find
   a the value of T when $z = 4$
   b the value of z when $T = 3 \cdot 6$.

3 Given that $y = \dfrac{k}{x}$, find the value of k and then copy and complete the table.

x	2	5		20
y	40		10	

4 Given that $s \propto \dfrac{1}{v^2}$, copy and complete the table.

v	3	4		
s	12		3	432

5 The electrical resistance, R, in a wire is inversely proportional
   to the square of the diameter, d. The resistance is $0 \cdot 36$ ohms
   when the diameter is $10\ \text{mm}$. Find the resistance when the
   diameter is $3\ \text{mm}$.

Homework 5H**C**

5.4 pages 261–264

1 Here are six curves, A, B, C, D, E and F.

A
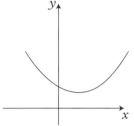

B
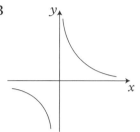

C
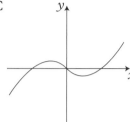

D
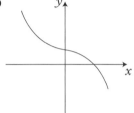

E
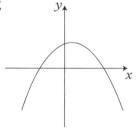

F
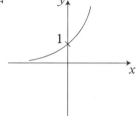

Here are the equations of the six curves, but they are not in the correct order.

1 $y = 6 + x - x^2$ **2** $y = 2^x$ **3** $y = 3 - x - 2x - x^3$

4 $y = x^3 - 4x$ **5** $y = \dfrac{4}{x}$ **6** $y = x^2 - 3x + 7$

Decide which equation fits each of the curves A to F.

2 Copy and complete the table for $y = x^2 + 5x$.

x	−2	−1	0	1	2	3
x^2					4	
5x					10	
y					14	

3 Copy and complete the table for $y = x^2 - 2x + 4$.

x	−3	−2	−1	0	1	2
x^2	9					
− 2x	6					
+4	4					
y	19					

Homework 5I ⊙

5.4 pages 264–265

For graphs use a scale of 2 cm for 1 unit on the x-axis and 1 cm to 1 unit on the y-axis.

1 a Copy and complete the table for $y = x^2 - 4$.

x	-3	-2	-1	0	1	2	3
x^2	9						
-4	-4	-4	-4				
y	5						

b Draw the graph of $y = x^2 - 4$ and use it to estimate
  i the x-values at $y = 3$
  ii the x-values at $y = -2$.

2 a Copy and complete the table for $y = x^2 + 3x$.

x	-4	-3	-2	-1	0	1
x^2						
$3x$						
y						

b Draw the graph of $y = x^2 + 3x$ and use it to estimate
  i the x-values at $y = 3$
  ii the x-values at $y = -1$.

3 Copy and complete the table for $y = x^2 + 2x - 3$.

x	-4	-3	-2	-1	0	1	2
x^2	16						
$2x$	-8						
-3	-3	-3	-3				
y	5						

Draw the graph of $y = x^2 + 2x - 3$, using axes with x from -4 to $+2$ and y from -4 to $+5$.

4 Copy and complete the table for $y = 2x^2 + x - 3$.
  [Remember that $2x^2 = 2(x^2)$.]

x	-3	-2	-1	0	1	2	3
$2x^2$	18						
x	-3						
-3	-3	-3	-3				
y	12						

Draw the graph of $y = 2x^2 + x - 3$, using axes with x from -3 to $+3$ and y from -4 to $+18$.

Homework 5J 🄲

5.5 page 271

1 The diagram shows the graphs of $y = x^2 + 2x - 1$ and $y = x + 3$.

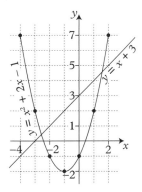

Use the graphs to find approximate solutions to these equations.
a $x^2 + 2x - 1 = x + 3$ **b** $x^2 + 2x - 1 = 0$

2 The diagram shows the graphs of $y = x^2 + x - 2$ and $y = x + 3$.

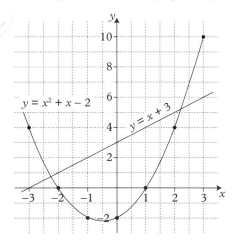

Use the graphs to find approximate solutions to these equations.
a $x^2 + x - 2 = x + 3$
b $x^2 + x - 2 = 3$
c $x^2 + x = 2$

3 a Draw the graphs of $y = x - 3$ and $y = x^2 - 7$ for values of x
from -3 to $+3$. Use scales of 1 cm to 1 unit on each
axis (as in question **1**).
b Use the graphs to find approximate solutions to the equation
$x^2 - x - 4 = 0$.

Homework 5K ⓔ

5.5 pages 270–274

1 The diagram shows the graphs
of $y = x^2 - 3x - 2$ and $y = 3 - x$.
Use the graphs to find approximate
solutions to these equations.
a $x^2 - 3x - 2 = 3 - x$
b $x^2 - 3x - 2 = 0$

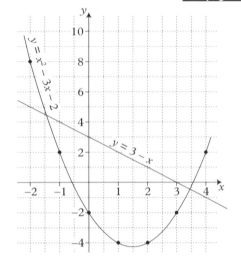

2 **a** Draw the graph of $y = x^2 - 2x - 1$ for values of x from -2 to $+4$.
   b Draw the graph of $y = 4 - x$ for the same values of x.
   c Use your graphs to find approximate solutions to these equations.
      i $x^2 - 2x - 1 = 4 - x$
      ii $x^2 - 2x - 1 = 0$

3 Use the graph to find approximate
solutions to these equations.
a $x^2 - 2x = x + 1$
b $x^2 - 2x = 0$
c $x^2 - 2x = 2$
d $x^2 - 2x = -1$

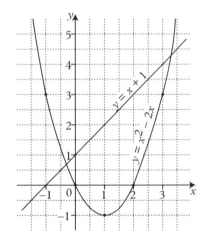

4 Assuming that the graph of $y = x^2 - 4x$ has
been drawn, find the equation of the line
which you would draw to solve these equations.
   a $x^2 - 4x = 6$ **b** $x^2 - 4x = -1$
   c $x^2 - 4x = x + 2$ **d** $x^2 - 5x = 0$
   e $x^2 - 5x + 1 = 0$

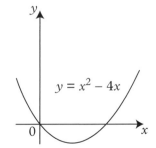

6 Shape, space and measures 2

Homework 6A C

6.1 pages 278–282

1 Which of these nets can you fold to make a cube?

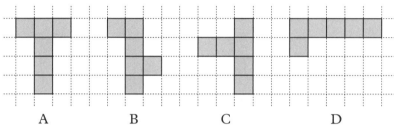

    A   B   C   D

2 Draw a net for this cuboid.

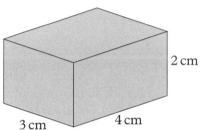

3 This is a diagram of a square-based pyramid.
VA = VB = VC = VD = 4 cm and AB = 3 cm.
Draw an accurate net for the pyramid.

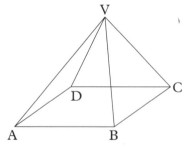

4 Use square grid paper to draw the plan view,
the front elevation and the side elevation
of the object shown.

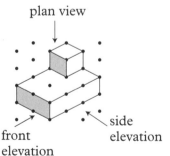

plan view

front
elevation

side
elevation

5 Here are two objects, A and B.
For each object, draw the
  a plan view
  b front elevation
  c side elevation.

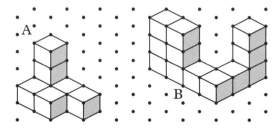

Homework 6B ❸

6.1 pages 282–284

For each shape state
a the number of lines of symmetry
b the order of rotational symmetry.

1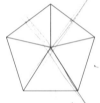

2

3

4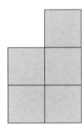

5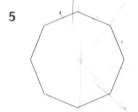

6

7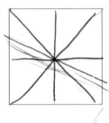

8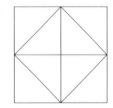

9

10 Here is a shape made using five squares.

Make seven copies of the diagram.
a Add one square so that the new shape has line symmetry.
 Do this in **four** different ways.
b Add one square so that the new shape has rotational symmetry
 of order 2. Do this in **two** different ways.

11 The diagram shows a cuboid. Draw two
 sketches of the cuboid and on each
 one draw a different plane of symmetry.

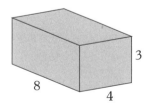

Homework 6C ©

6.2 pages 285–288

In each question, find the length of the side marked with a letter.

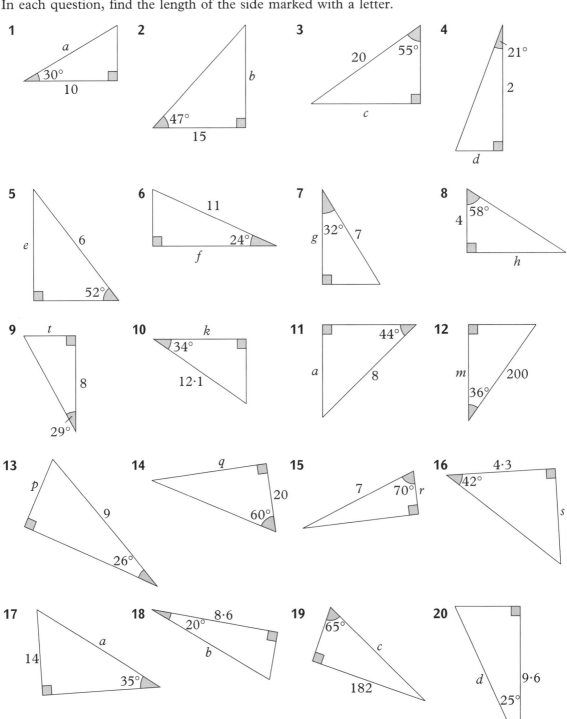

Homework 6D ⓒ

6.2 pages 289–290

Find the angles marked with letters.

1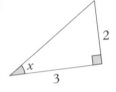

2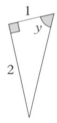

3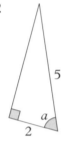

4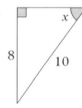

5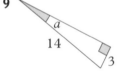

6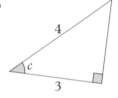

7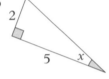

8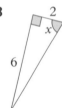

9

10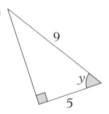

11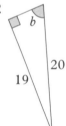

12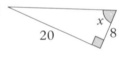

13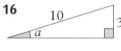

14

15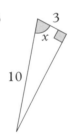

16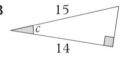

17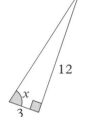

18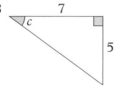

19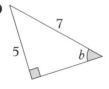

20

21 Work out the size of the smallest angle in a right-angled triangle with sides of length 10 m, 24 m and 26 m.

22 Calculate the acute angle between the diagonals of a rectangle with sides 8 cm and 13 cm.

Homework 6E⊙ Mixed questions

6.2 pages 285–289

In each question, find the length or the angle that is marked with a letter.

1

2

3

4

5

6

7

8

9

10

11

12

13

14

15

16

17 Rectangle ABCD lies in a horizontal plane and point E is vertically above C.
AB = 10 m, AD = 7 m and EC = 5 m.
Find these angles.
  a EDC **b** ECB **c** CAE

Homework 6F🕒

6.2 pages 297–299

1 The diagram shows a cuboid.
Find
  a BD
  b BN
  c the angle NBD.

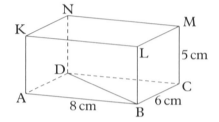

2 The diagram shows a square-based
pyramid in which V is vertically
above the centre of the base.
AB = AD = 8 cm and VC = 10 cm.
Find
  a VE
  b the angle between VC and the plane ABCD.

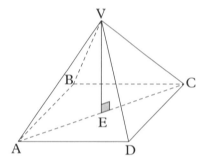

3 The diagram shows a cuboid.
Calculate the angle between AR
and the plane ABCD.

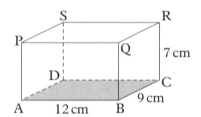

4 In the diagram the plane ABCD is horizontal.
Find
  a EC
  b angle EBC.

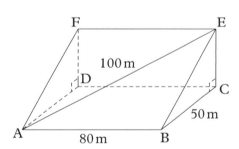

5 The diagram shows a cube of
side 8 cm with a diagonal PQ.
Find the angle between PQ and
the base of the cube.

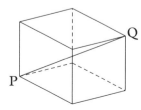

Homework 6G $\textcircled{c}$

6.3 pages 300–303

1 State whether these quantities are lengths, areas, volumes or none of these.

  a 8 km   **b** $3 \cdot 2 \text{ m}^3$
  c the perimeter of a square   **d** 32 m/s
  e 800 cm^2 **f** $2\pi \text{ cm}^3$
  g the radius of a circle   **h** the radius of a sphere
  i the weight of a can   **j** the value of a CD
  k the number of inches in a foot   **l** 10 litres
  m 4 tonnes   **n** the girth of a tree
  o the power of a motor   **p** the amount of jam in a jar

2 The symbols a, b, c, h, r and p represent lengths. State the number of dimensions (L, L^2, L^3) for each of these.

  a $2ab$ **b** b^2c **c** $3\pi r$
  d a^2h **e** $3(2h + p)$ **f** $r^3 + ab^2$
  g $8ab + a^2$ **h** $\dfrac{\pi h^3}{4}$ **i** $(r + p)^2$

3 Paul worked out the formula for the volume of an object as

$$\boxed{V = \pi a^2 b + ra^2 + b^2}$$

Explain why this cannot be correct.

4 The symbols a, b, c and r represent lengths and θ represents an angle. For each expression state whether it represents length, L, area, A or volume, V, or mixed dimensions, MD.

  a $ab - c^2$ **b** $5a + 7c$ **c** $a^2 + a^3$
  d $\pi r^2 + ab$ **e** $\dfrac{(a + b)^2}{4}$ **f** $\dfrac{1}{2}ab \sin \theta$
  g $\pi a + ac$ **h** $a^2 \cos \theta$ **i** $\dfrac{(a + b)^2}{2r}$

5 Which of these could represent an area and which could represent a volume?

$$\boxed{\dfrac{1}{2}ab \sin 40° + a^2} \qquad \boxed{\dfrac{(a + b)^2}{c}} \qquad \boxed{\dfrac{(a^3 + b^3)}{a}} \qquad \boxed{\pi r^3 + bc \cos \theta}$$

Homework 6H❻ Reflection and rotation

6.4 pages 303–305

1 Copy the diagram.
Draw the image of △ABC after reflection in
  a the *y*-axis; label it △1
  b the *x*-axis; label it △2
  c the line *y* = 1; label it △3
  d the line *y* = *x*; label it △4.
Write the coordinates of the image of
the point A in each case.

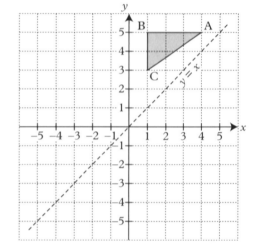

For questions **2**, **3** and **4** draw a set of axes for *x* and *y* from −8 to +8.

2 Plot and label G(8, 7), H(8, 3), I(6, 3).
Draw the image of △GHI after reflection in
  a the line *y* = 3; label it △1
  b the *x*-axis; label it △2
  c the line *x* = 2; label it △3
  d the *y*-axis; label it △4
  e the line *y* = *x*; label it △5
  f the line *y* = −*x*; label it △6.
Write the coordinates of the image of the point G in each case.

3 Plot and label K(2, 5), L(2, 8), M(4, 8). Draw the image of △KLM
after the rotation
  a 90° clockwise, centre (0, 0); label it △1
  b 90° anticlockwise, centre (0, 0); label it △2
  c 180° centre (4, 4); label it △3
  d 90° clockwise, centre (−4, 2); label it △4
  e 90° anticlockwise, centre (4, 0); label it △5.
Write the coordinates of the image of the point K in each case.

4 Plot and label P(−3, −4), Q(−5, −6), R(−3, −7). Draw the image
of △PQR after the rotation
  a 90° clockwise, centre (0, 0); label it △1.
  b 90° anticlockwise, centre (0, 0); label it △2
  c 180°, centre (−4, −4); label it △3
  d 90° anticlockwise, centre (−4, 4); label it △4
  e 180°, centre (−2, 0); label it △5
Write the coordinates of the image of the point P in each case.

Homework 61 C Enlargement and translation

6.4 pages 305–309

1 Copy the diagram.
Draw the image of △ABC after the enlargement
a scale factor 2, centre (0, 0); label it △1
b scale factor 2, centre (4, 2); label it △2
c scale factor 3, centre (2, 3); label it △3
d scale factor 2, centre (−1, 5); label it △4.
Write the coordinates of the image of the
point A in each case.

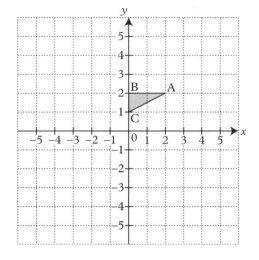

For questions **2** and **3** draw axes for x and y from −8 to +8.

2 Plot and label D(2, 1), E(2, 3), F(1, 3).
Draw the image of △DEF after the enlargement
a scale factor 2, centre (0, 0); label it △1
b scale factor 2, centre (0, 8); label it △2
c scale factor −2, centre (2, 0); label it △3
d Draw the image of △3 after enlargement
with scale factor $\frac{1}{2}$, centre (−2, −4); label it △4.
e Describe the transformation which moves △4
onto △DEF.

3 Plot and label K(5, 1), L(1, 1), M(2, 4). Draw the image of △KLM
after the translation

a $\begin{pmatrix} 3 \\ 4 \end{pmatrix}$; label it △1

b $\begin{pmatrix} 3 \\ -4 \end{pmatrix}$; label it △2

c $\begin{pmatrix} -5 \\ 4 \end{pmatrix}$; label it △3

d $\begin{pmatrix} -8 \\ -7 \end{pmatrix}$; label it △4

e $\begin{pmatrix} -9 \\ 0 \end{pmatrix}$; label it △5.

Write the coordinates of the image of the point K in
each case.

Homework 6J⊙ Describing transformations

6.4 pages 303–311

For each question draw axes for x and y from -8 to 8.

1 Plot and label these triangles

△1:   (4, 2)   (8, 2)   (8, 4).

Shade triangle 1.

△2: (−4, 2)   (−8, 2)   (−8, 4)
△3: (−2, 4)   (−2, 8)   (−4, 8)
△4: (0, −3)   (8, −3)   (8, 1)
△5: (−4, −2) (−8, −2) (−8, −4)
△6: (2, 4)   (2, 8)   (4, 8)

Describe fully these transformations

a △1→△2   **b** △1→△3
c △1→△4   **d** △1→△5
e △1→△6   **f** △2→△5

2 Plot and label these triangles

△1:   (4, −3)   (7, −3)   (7, −5).

Shade triangle 1.

△2: (−4, 3)   (5, 3)   (5, −3)
△3: (4, 5)   (7, 5)   (7, 7)
△4: (−5, −3) (−2, −3) (−2, −5)
△5: (−2, 3)   (−5, 3)   (−5, 5)
△6: (−6, −1) (−6, −4) (−8, −4)

Describe fully these transformations

a △1→△2   **b** △1→△3
c △1→△4   **d** △1→△5
e △1→△6   **f** △4→△5

3 a Plot and label L(1, 5), M(1, 1), N(3, 1).
  b Draw the image of △LMN after reflection in $x = 0$ followed by reflection in $y = x$. Label the image △1.
  c Describe the single transformation △LMN on to △1.
  d Draw the image of △LMN after rotation 180° about $(-1, -1)$ followed by translation $\begin{pmatrix} 4 \\ 4 \end{pmatrix}$. Label the image △2.
  e Describe the single transformation △LMN onto △2.
  f Describe the single transformation △1 onto △2.

Homework 6K ⓒ

6.5 pages 311–315

1 Write each vector in terms of **a** or **b** or **a** and **b**.

a

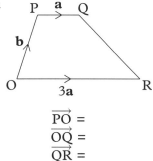

$\overrightarrow{PO} =$
$\overrightarrow{OQ} =$
$\overrightarrow{QR} =$

b

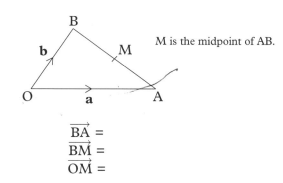

M is the midpoint of AB.

$\overrightarrow{BA} =$
$\overrightarrow{BM} =$
$\overrightarrow{OM} =$

c

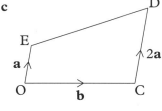

$\overrightarrow{EC} =$
$\overrightarrow{ED} =$
$\overrightarrow{OD} =$

d

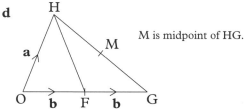

M is midpoint of HG.

$\overrightarrow{HG} =$
$\overrightarrow{HM} =$
$\overrightarrow{OM} =$
$\overrightarrow{GH} =$

2 ABCD is a parallelogram with $\overrightarrow{AB}$ = **a** and $\overrightarrow{AD}$ = **b**.
M is the midpoint of AD and AP : PC = 1 : 2.
Find these vectors in terms of **a** and **b**.
a $\overrightarrow{AC}$
b $\overrightarrow{AP}$
c $\overrightarrow{MP}$
d $\overrightarrow{PB}$
Hence show that the points M, P and B lie on a straight line.

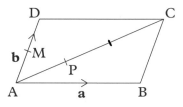

Homework 6L⒠

6.5 pages 315–317

1 Write each vector in terms of **a** or **b** or **a** and **b**.

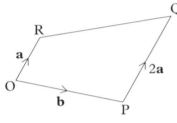

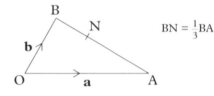

$\overrightarrow{RP}$ =
$\overrightarrow{OQ}$ =
$\overrightarrow{RQ}$ =

$\overrightarrow{BA}$ =
$\overrightarrow{BN}$ =
$\overrightarrow{ON}$ =

2 In the diagram, P is the midpoint of AB
and M is the midpoint of AP.
$\overrightarrow{OA} = \mathbf{a}$ and $\overrightarrow{OB} = \mathbf{b}$
Write these vectors in terms of **a** and **b**.

a $\overrightarrow{AB}$

b $\overrightarrow{AM}$

c $\overrightarrow{OM}$

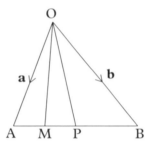

3 OPQR is a quadrilateral in which $\overrightarrow{OP} = \mathbf{a}$, $\overrightarrow{PQ} = \mathbf{b}$ and $\overrightarrow{OR} = 2\mathbf{b}$.
M is the midpoint of PR and S is the point such that OPSR is a
parallelogram.
a What type of quadrilateral is OPQR?
b Find $\overrightarrow{OS}$ in terms of **a** and **b**.
c Find $\overrightarrow{PR}$ in terms of **a** and **b**.
d Find $\overrightarrow{OM}$ in terms of **a** and **b**.

4 In the diagram $\overrightarrow{OD} = 2\overrightarrow{OA}$, $\overrightarrow{OE} = 4\overrightarrow{OB}$, $\overrightarrow{OA} = \mathbf{a}$ and $\overrightarrow{OB} = \mathbf{b}$.
a Express in terms of **a** and **b**

  i $\overrightarrow{OD}$ **ii** $\overrightarrow{OE}$ **iii** $\overrightarrow{BA}$ **iv** $\overrightarrow{ED}$

b Given that $\overrightarrow{BC} = 3\overrightarrow{BA}$, express $\overrightarrow{OC}$ in terms of **a** and **b**.
c Express $\overrightarrow{EC}$ in terms of **a** and **b**.
d Hence show that the points E, D and C lie on a straight line.

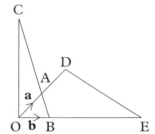

Homework 6M Ⓔ

6.6 pages 319–321

1 Sketch the graphs of these functions.
   a $y = \sin x$ for $0 \leqslant x \leqslant 360°$
   b $y = \cos x$ for $0 \leqslant x \leqslant 360°$
   c $y = \tan x$ for $0 \leqslant x \leqslant 360°$

2 Use your graphs from question **1** to sort these into pairs
   of equal value. Do not use a calculator.

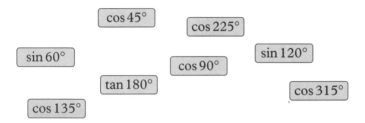

In questions **3** to **6** give the angles correct to one decimal
place.

3 If $\sin x = 0{\cdot}5$, find two values for x between $0°$ and $360°$.

4 If $\sin x = 0{\cdot}7$, find two values for x between $0°$ and $360°$.

5 If $\tan x = 2$, find two values for x between $0°$ and $360°$.

6 If $\cos x = 0{\cdot}45$, find two values for x between $0°$ and $360°$.

7 Sort these into pairs of equal value. Do not use a calculator.

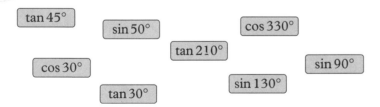

Homework 6N Ⓔ

6.7 pages 323–326

Reminder	$\dfrac{a}{\sin A} = \dfrac{b}{\sin B} = \dfrac{c}{\sin C}$

In questions **1** to **6** find the sides marked with letters correct to
2 decimal places. All lengths are in cm.

1

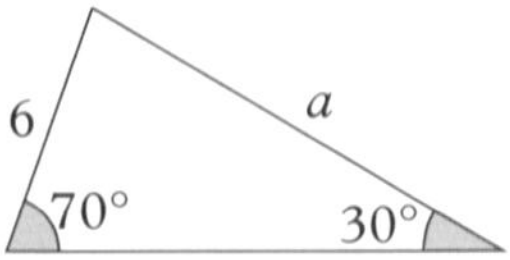

6   a 70°   30°

2

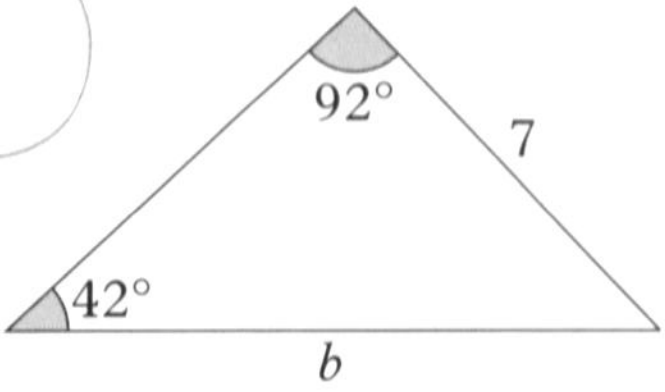

92°   7   42° b

3

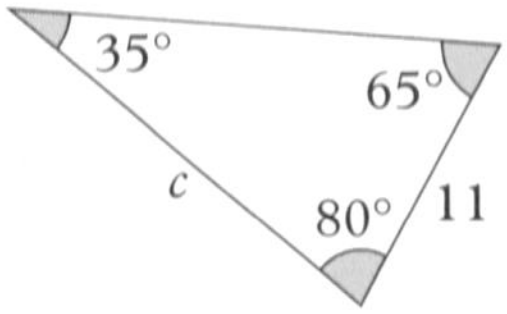

35°   65° c 80°   11

4

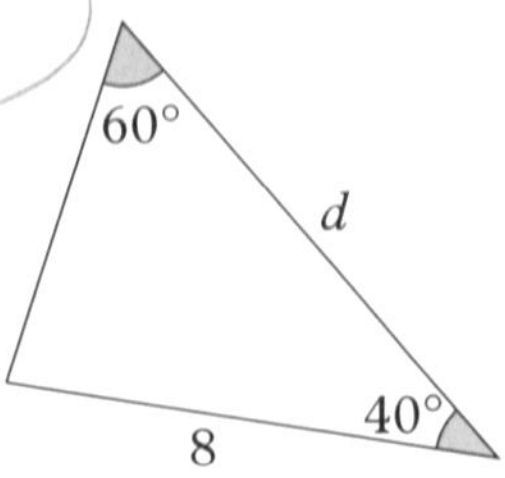

60° d 8   40°

5

32°   125° e 6·5

6

12   f 40° f

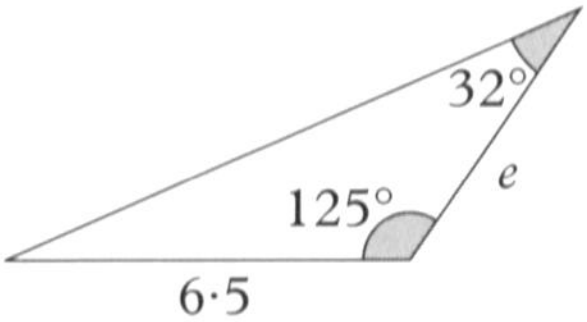

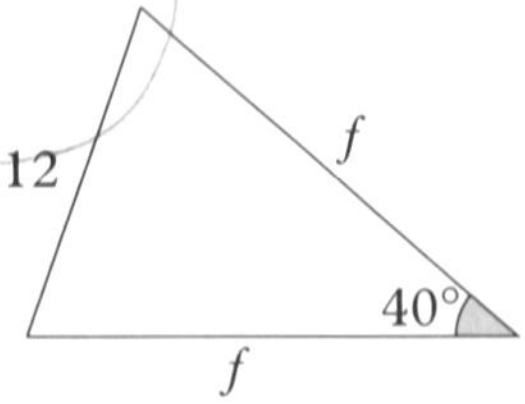

7 In triangle LMN, ∠L = 53°, ∠N = 74° and MN = 5·2 cm.
Find the length of LM, correct to 2 decimal places.

In questions **8** to **13** find the angles marked with letters. All lengths
are in cm.

8

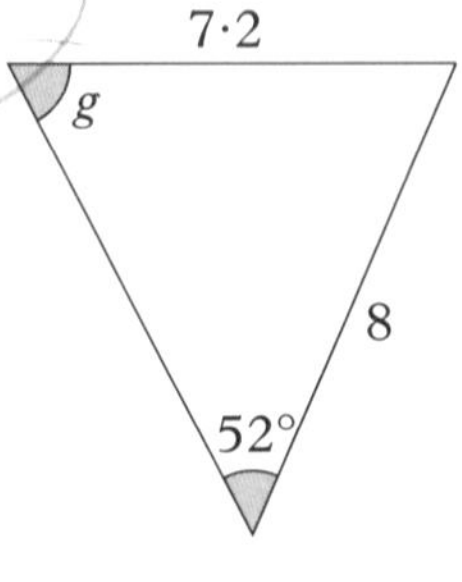

7·2 g 8   52°

9

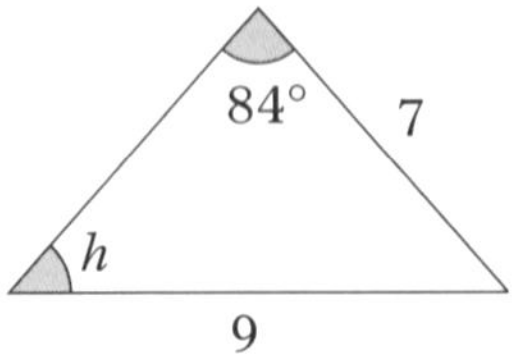

84°   7 h 9

10

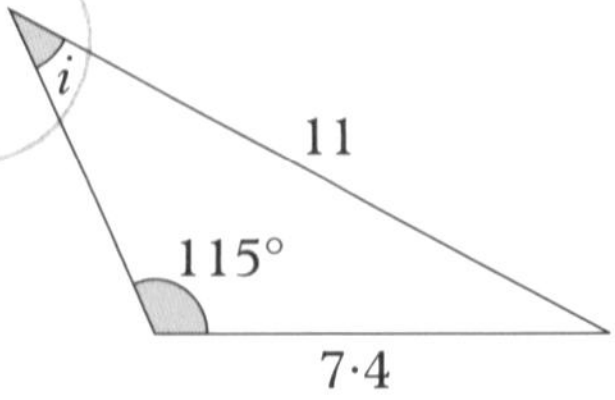

i 11   115°   7·4

11

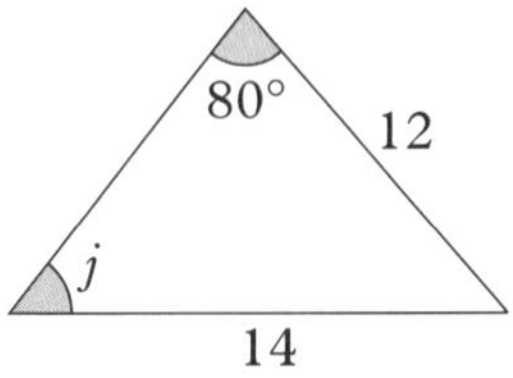

80°   12 j 14

12

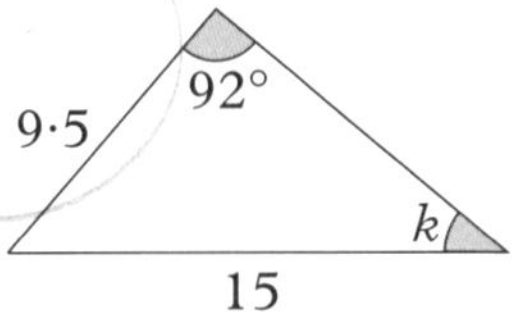

9·5   92° k 15

13

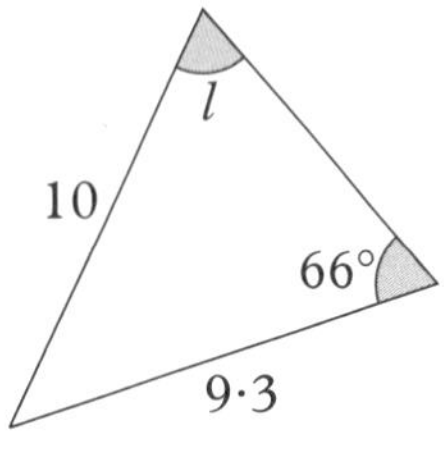

l 10   66°   9·3

Homework 6O Ⓔ

6.7 pages 326–332

Reminder $a^2 = b^2 + c^2 - 2bc\cos A$

In questions **1** to **5** find the sides marked with letters, giving your answers correct to 2 decimal places. All lengths are in cm.

1
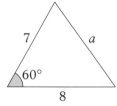

2
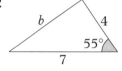

3
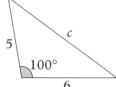

4
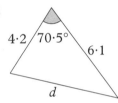

5
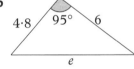

In questions **6** to **8** find the angles marked with letters.
All lengths are in cm.

6
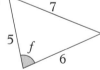

7
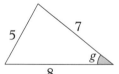

8
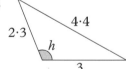

In questions **9** to **11** decide whether you need the cosine rule or the sine rule.
Find the angles and sides marked with letters. All lengths are in cm.

9
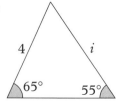

10
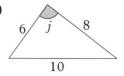

11
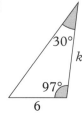

Homework 6PⒺ

6.7 page 329

1 a Calculate the area of triangle ABC.
  b Calculate the perimeter of the triangle.

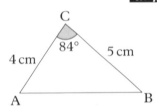

2 Two ships, X and Y, leave a port P at 12:00 hours.
  Ship X travels on a bearing of 125° at a speed of 15 km per hour.
  Ship Y travels on a bearing of 200° at a speed of 18 km per hour.
  a Draw a diagram showing X, Y and P at 14:00 hours.
  b Calculate the distance between X and Y at 14:00 hours.

3 A circle centre O has radius 10 cm.
  BC is a tangent to the circle at B.
  Points A, O and C lie on a straight line.
  BC = 20 cm.
  Calculate   **a** angle COB
           b angle ABC.

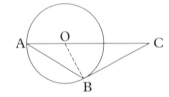

4 The area of triangle PQR is 12·2 cm². Calculate
  the length PR correct to three significant figures.

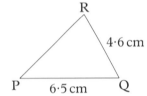

Homework 6QⒺ

6.7 pages 318–332

1 a Sketch the graph of $y = \sin x$ for $0 \leqslant x \leqslant 360°$.
  b You are given that $\sin 18° = 0·309$.
    i Solve the equation
      $\sin x = 0·309$ for $0 \leqslant x \leqslant 360°$
    ii State a solution to the equation
      $\sin (x - 20°) = 0·309$

2 D is the point of AC such that angle BDA = 90°.
  Calculate the length of BD.

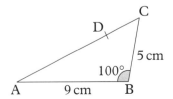

3 a Work out the length KM correct to 3 significant figures.
  b KLM and KMN are similar triangles in which
    angle LKM = angle MKN.
  Calculate the length KN.

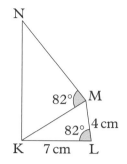

4 A parallelogram has sides 8 cm and 13 cm and angles
68° and 112°.
  a Calculate the length of the shorter diagonal of
    the parallelogram.
  b Calculate the area of the parallelogram.

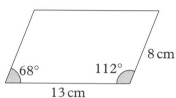

Homework 6R Ⓔ

6.8 pages 333–334

Find the angles marked with letters. O is the centre of the circle.

1   **2** 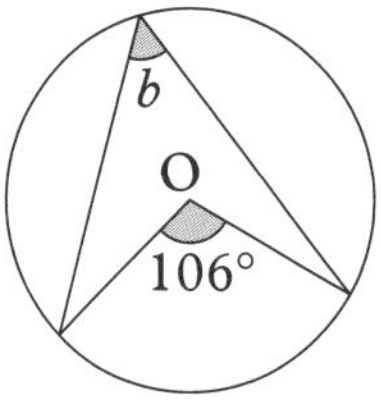   **3** 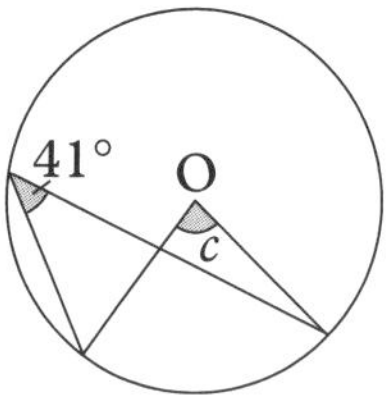   **4**

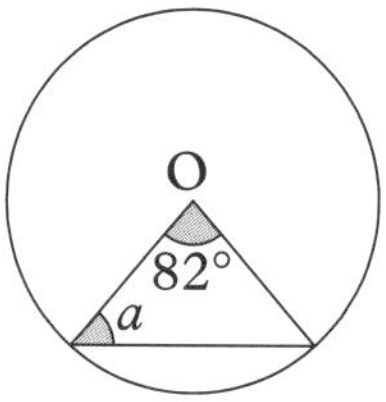

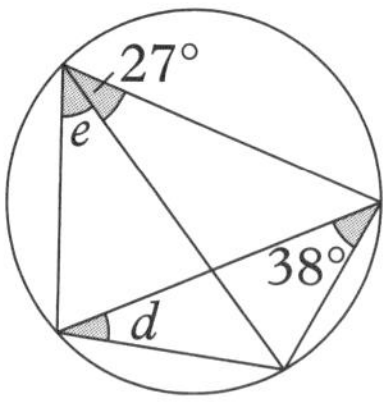

5 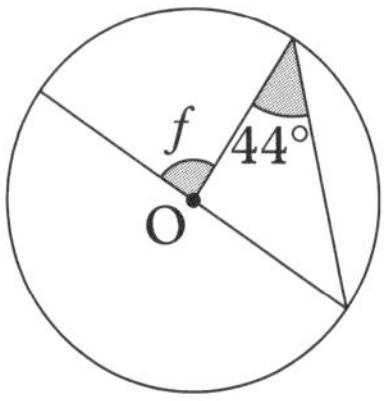   **6** 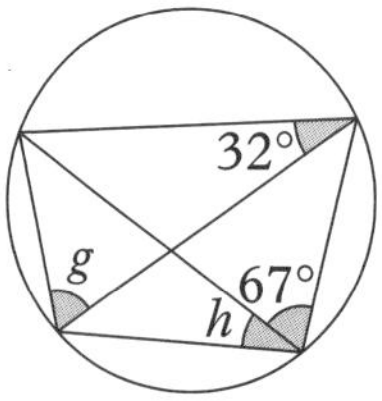   **7** 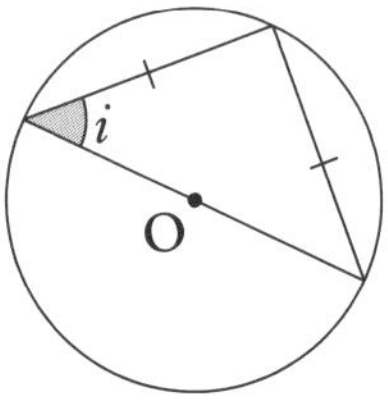   **8**

9 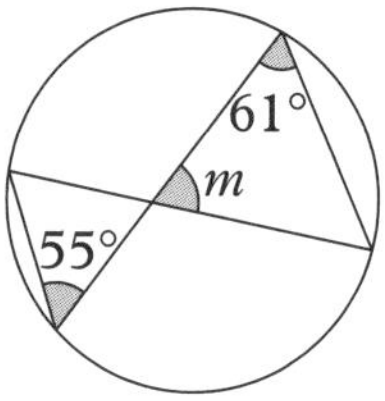   **10** 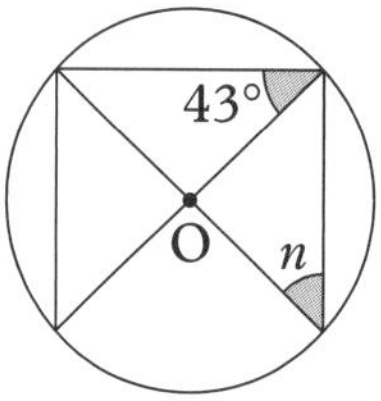   **11** 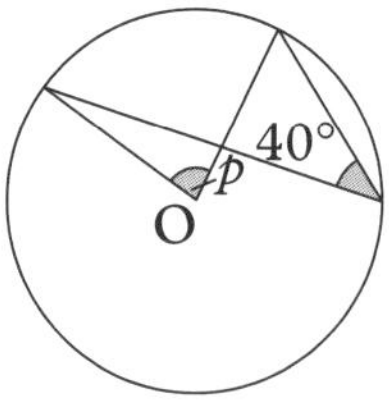   **12**

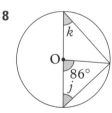

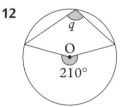

13 In the diagram AB = BC and angle ABC = 108°.
Find angle BDC and write the reason for
each step in your working.

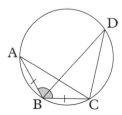

14 Find these angles.

   a ∠PQS

   b ∠POS

   c ∠PSO

   Write the reasons for your answers.

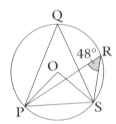

Homework 6SⒺ

6.8 pages 333–336

Find the angles marked with letters. O is the centre of the circle.

1

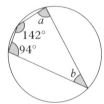

2

3

4

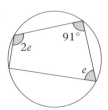

5

6

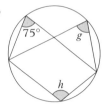

7

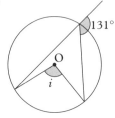

8

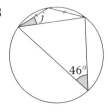

9

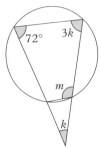

10 In this question give reasons for your answers.

   a Find angle CBA.

   b Find angle BCA.

   c Find angle AOB.

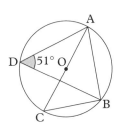

Homework 6TE

6.8 pages 337–339

Find the angles marked with letters. Point O is the centre of the circle.

1

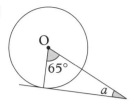

2

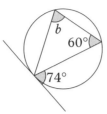

3

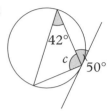

4

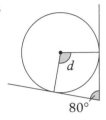

5

6

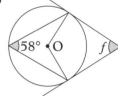

7

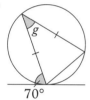

8

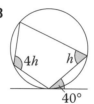

9

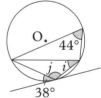

10 a Find angle QOR.
    b Find angle PRO.
    Give reasons for your answers.

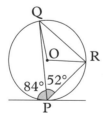

7   Algebra 3

Homework 7A❻

7.1 pages 347–352

1 Find the value of

    a 4^2 **b** 3^3 **c** 7^0 **d** 10^4

2 Write in a simpler form.

    a $6^2 \times 6^4$ **b** $7^5 \times 7^3$ **c** $3^6 \div 3^2$ **d** $7^{10} \div 7^3$

3 Write these as either fractions or integers.

    a 8^{-1} **b** 2^{-2} **c** 3^{-1} **d** $9^{\frac{1}{2}}$

    e 5×4^0 **f** $16^{-\frac{1}{2}}$ **g** half of 2^5 **h** $1000^{\frac{1}{3}}$

4 Simplify.

    a $n^2 \times n^5$ **b** $x^9 \div x^2$ **c** $\dfrac{n^4 \times n^5}{n^3}$ **d** $\dfrac{m}{m^7}$

    e $(a^2)^3$ **f** $(2n^2)^2$ **g** $(y^3)^4$ **h** $b^{-2} \times b^3$

5 The sketch shows points on
the curve $y = 9^x$.
Find the values of p, q, r, and s.

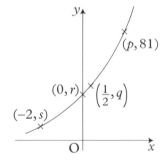

6 Evaluate.

    a $169^{\frac{1}{2}}$ **b** $49^{-0.5} \times 49^{\frac{1}{2}}$ **c** $8^{\frac{2}{3}}$ **d** $9^{\frac{3}{2}}$

    e $36^{\frac{1}{2}} \times 6^{-1}$ **f** $4x^0$ **g** $(4x)^0$ **h** $100^{-\frac{1}{2}} \times 1^3$

7 Given that $n > 1$ write in ascending order

    n^{-1}, n^3, $n^{\frac{1}{2}}$, n^0

8 You are given that $x = 3^a$ and $y = 3^b$.
Express in terms of x and/or y

    a 3^{a+b} **b** 3^{2a}

Homework 7B C

7.1 pages 349–352

1 a Express $\dfrac{6}{\sqrt{3}}$ in the form $a\sqrt{b}$, where a and b are integers.

 b Rationalise $\dfrac{1}{\sqrt{2}}$. ('rationalise' means write with an integer denominator)

 c Rationalise $\dfrac{10}{\sqrt{5}}$.

2 Evaluate.
 a $(2\sqrt{2})^2$ **b** $(2\sqrt{5})^2$ **c** $(\sqrt{2} + \sqrt{8})^2$

3 Write these in the form $a\sqrt{b}$, where a and b are integers.
 a $\sqrt{12}$ **b** $\sqrt{50}$ **c** $\sqrt{48}$

4 Find the area of the rectangle, giving your answer as an integer.

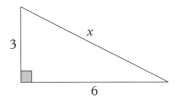

$\dfrac{3}{\sqrt{2}}$ cm

$\dfrac{6}{\sqrt{2}}$ cm

5 a Write $16^{\frac{1}{2}} \times 4^{-2}$ in the form 2^a.

 b Write $9^{\frac{3}{2}} \times 3^{-2}$ in the form 3^b.

6 Find x.
 Express your answer in the form $n\sqrt{5}$,
 where n is an integer.

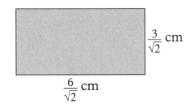

7 Here are three curves with equations $y = 2^x$, $y = 2^{\frac{5}{2}}$ and $y = 2^{-x}$, but not
 in that order. Decide which equation fits each curve.

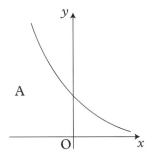

A

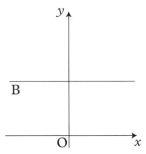

B

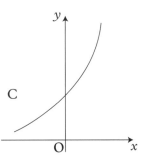

C

Homework 7C ⊙

7.2 pages 352–355

1 a Solve $3(2x - 1) = 5(2 - x)$.   **b** Factorise $2a^2 + 6ab$.   **c** Factorise $6mn^2 - 3mn$.

2 Expand and simplify.

   a $(n + 3)(n + 4)$ **b** $(n + 5)(n - 2)$ **c** $(2n + 1)(n + 3)$

3 Factorise these expressions.

   a $x^2 + 5x + 6$ **b** $x^2 + 5x + 4$ **c** $x^2 + 11x + 28$

   d $x^2 - 3x - 10$ **e** $x^2 - 7x + 6$ **f** $x^2 - 14x + 24$

   g $x^2 - 4x - 21$ **h** $x^2 - x - 20$ **i** $x^2 + 19x + 48$

4 The area of each rectangle is written in terms of n. Factorise the expression and hence find the perimeter of the rectangle in terms of n.

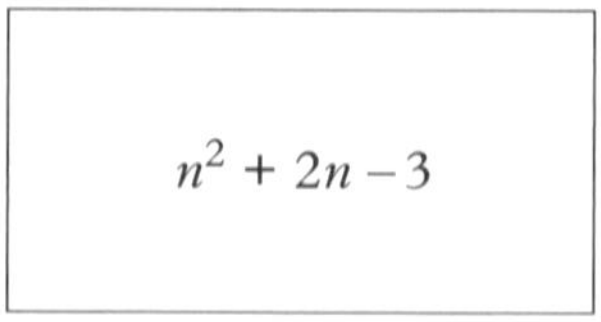

$$n^2 + 2n - 3$$

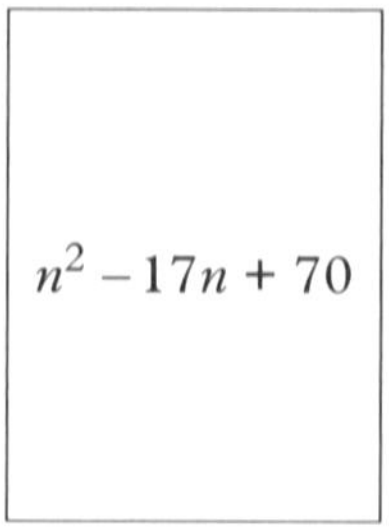

$$n^2 - 17n + 70$$

5 Simplify.

   a $\dfrac{2x^2 - 2x}{x^2 - 1}$ **b** $\dfrac{x^2 + x - 12}{x^2 + 4x}$ **c** $\dfrac{x^2 - 9}{x^2 - 5x + 6}$

6 Factorise $(a + b)^2 + 3(a + b)$.

7 The perimeter of the rectangle in the diagram is $(4x + 2)$ cm. Find an expression for the area of the rectangle, in terms of x.

$(x + 3)$ cm

Homework 7D

7.2 pages 355–357

1 Expand and simplify.

   a $(2x + 1)(x + 2)$ **b** $(3x + 2)(x - 1)$ **c** $(2x - 3)^2$

2 a Simplify $(2x^2y)^3$.   **b** Solve $(x + 3)(x - 1) = (x + 5)(x - 1)$.

   c Factorise $6a^3b - 15a^2b^2$.

3 Factorise these expressions.

   a $2x^2 + 11x + 5$ **b** $3x^2 + 8x + 4$ **c** $4x^2 + 8x + 3$

   d $2x^2 + 5x + 3$ **e** $2x^2 - x - 15$ **f** $5x^2 + 8x + 3$

4 Factorise fully.

   a $x^2 - a^2$ **b** $n^2 - p^2$ **c** $x^2 - 4$

   d $n^3 - n$ **e** $2x^2 - 50$ **f** $p^3 - pq^2$

5 Solve these equations.

a $x(x - 3) = 0$ **b** $(x + 2)(x - 5) = 0$ **c** $x^2 + 7x + 12 = 0$

d $x^2 + 5x - 14 = 0$ **e** $2x^2 - x - 3 = 0$ **f** $6x^2 + x - 2 = 0$

6 Simplify.

a $\dfrac{2x^2 + 7x - 4}{x^2 - 16}$ **b** $\dfrac{6x^2 + 11x - 10}{3x^2 + x - 2}$ **c** $\dfrac{12x^2 + 5x - 3}{6x^2 - 2x}$

7 The area of this rectangle is 56 square units.
Form an equation and solve it to find the value of x.

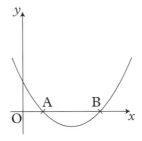

$x + 4$

$3x - 1$

8 The curve $y = 6x^2 - 11x + 4$ crosses
the x-axis at the points A and B.
Find the coordinates of A and B.

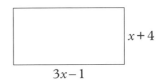

Homework 7E

7.2 pages 357–360

1 a Solve the equation $x^2 + 4x = 21$. **b** Simplify $\dfrac{x^2 - 16}{x^2 + 4x}$.

  c Solve $(2x + 1)(2x - 3) = 4x(x - 3)$.

2 Solve these equations, giving answers correct to two decimal places.

  a $2x^2 + 5x + 1 = 0$ **b** $3x^2 + x - 5 = 0$ **c** $x(2x - 5) = 1$

3 Two numbers have a difference of 7 and a product of 31·31.

  a If the larger number is n. Show that **b** Solve the equation
  $n^2 - 7n - 31 \cdot 31 = 0$ $n^2 - 7n - 31 \cdot 31 = 0$

4 The curve $y = 2x^2$ meets the line
$y = 5x + 3$.
Find the x-coordinates of the
points A and B.

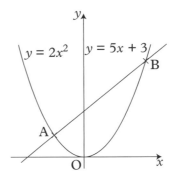

5 The diagonals of this rectangle are of length 17 units.
Form an equation and solve it to find x.

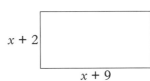

$x + 2$

$x + 9$

Homework 7F ◉

7.2 pages 361–363

1 a Simplify $(2x - 1)^2 - 3$.

   b Write as a single fraction $\dfrac{1}{x} + \dfrac{1}{x + 1}$.

2 Write each expression in the form $(x + a)^2 + b$.

   a $x^2 + 8x + 20$ **b** $x^2 + 6x + 2$ **c** $x^2 + 10x$

3 Solve these equations by completing the square. Where necessary leave your answer in a form involving a surd (such as $\sqrt{2}$).

   a $x^2 + 8x + 12 = 0$ **b** $x^2 + 10x + 16 = 0$

   c $x^2 + 2x - 2 = 0$ **d** $x^2 - 4x - 1 = 0$

4 The curve $y = (x - 3)^2 + 2$ crosses the y-axis at A and has a minimum point at B.

Find the coordinates of the points A and B.

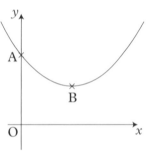

5 a Write $x^2 + 2x + 5$ in the form $(x + a)^2 + b$, where a and b are integers.

   b Hence draw a sketch of the curve $y = x^2 + 2x + 5$, indicating the coordinates of the minimum point on the curve.

6 a Find the integers a and b if $x^2 + 8x + a = (x + b)^2$

   b Write $2x^2 + 2x + 1$ in the form $a(x + b)^2 + c$, where a, b and c are either integers or fractions.

Homework 7G ◉

7.3 pages 367–369

1 Simplify these expressions as far as possible.

   a $\dfrac{5n^2}{2n}$ **b** $\dfrac{a}{3a}$ **c** $\dfrac{x^2 + 2x}{2x}$ **d** $\dfrac{4n + 2}{2n}$

   e $\dfrac{6ab}{2b^2}$ **f** $\dfrac{x(x - 2)}{x^2 - 4}$ **g** $\dfrac{9x + 3}{6x}$ **h** $\dfrac{12ab}{8ba}$

2 Write these as single fractions in their simplest form.

   a $\dfrac{3n}{7} \times \dfrac{14}{n}$ **b** $\dfrac{x}{2} \times \dfrac{x + 1}{x}$ **c** $\dfrac{x}{4} \div \dfrac{x}{2}$

   d $\left(\dfrac{a}{3}\right)^2 \times \dfrac{3}{a}$ **e** $\dfrac{5}{z} \div \dfrac{x}{2}$ **f** $\dfrac{(x + 1)^2}{2} \times \dfrac{4}{x^2 - 1}$

3 Solve $\dfrac{x}{2x-1} = 3$.

4 Write as single fractions and give your answers in their simplest form.

a $\dfrac{1}{2} + \dfrac{1}{3}$ **b** $\dfrac{1}{x} + \dfrac{2}{x}$ **c** $\dfrac{2}{3} + \dfrac{1}{x}$

d $\dfrac{1}{x} + \dfrac{1}{x+2}$ **e** $\dfrac{x}{x+1} - \dfrac{1}{x}$ **f** $\dfrac{x+1}{x+2} + \dfrac{x}{x-2}$

5 Solve $\dfrac{x}{x-1} + \dfrac{3}{x+1} = 3$

6 Solve $\dfrac{12}{x+2} + \dfrac{2}{x-2} = \dfrac{36}{x^2-4}$

*7 The diagram shows the circle with equation $x^2 + y^2 = 9$ and
the line $y = x - 2$.
  a Show that the x-coordinates of points P and Q are given by the
  solutions to the equation $2x^2 - 4x - 5 = 0$
  b Solve the equation $2x^2 - 4x - 5 = 0$, giving your solutions
  correct to 2 decimal places.

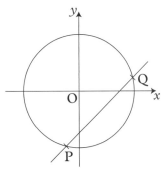

Homework 7H

7.4 pages 369–372

1 The diagram shows the graph of $y = x^2$.

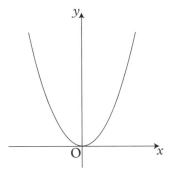

Find the equation of each of these graphs.

a

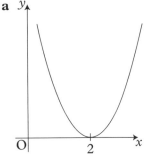

b

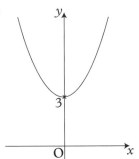

c

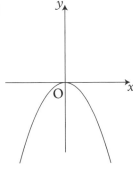

2 This is the graph of $y = f(x)$.

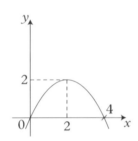

Sketch these functions on similar diagrams.
a $y = f(x + 2)$ **b** $y = f(x) - 2$ **c** $y = 2f(x)$

3 This is the graph of $y = f(x)$.
Draw sketch graphs of these functions.
a $y = f(x - 1)$
b $y = f(x) + 2$
c $y = f(2x)$

4 The diagram shows the graph of $y = \cos x$.
For $0° \leqslant x \leqslant 360°$.
Sketch the graph of

a $y = \cos\left(\dfrac{x}{2}\right)$ for $0° \leqslant x \leqslant 360°$

b $y = \cos(x - 90°)$ for $0° \leqslant x \leqslant 360°$.

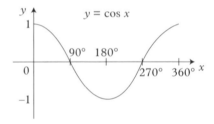

Homework 71Ⓔ

7.4 pages 369–376

1 This is the graph of $y = f(x)$.
Sketch these graphs.
a $y = f(x - 3)$
b $y = f(2x)$
Give the new coordinates of point A on each graph.

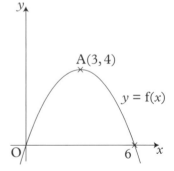

2 This is a sketch of the curve $y = \sin x$ for $0° \leqslant x \leqslant 360°$.
Sketch the following for $0 \leqslant x \leqslant 360$
a $y = \sin x + 1$
b $y = \sin\left(\dfrac{x}{2}\right)$

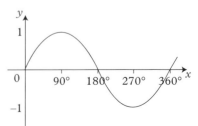

3 The diagram shows the graph of $y = g(x)$.

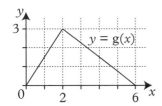

Find the functions for these graphs.

a

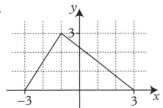

b

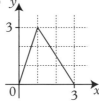

c

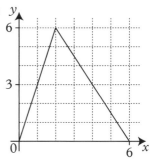

4 a Show that $f(x) = x^2 - 6x + 11$ can be written in the form
$f(x) = (x - 3)^2 + 2$.
b Hence or otherwise draw a sketch of the graph $y = f(x)$, giving the coordinates of the minimum point of the curve.
c Sketch the graph of
   i $y = f(x) - 2$ **ii** $y = -f(x)$

8 Handling data

Homework 8A Ⓒ

8.1 pages 380–386

1 a Calculate the mean of 3, 3, 5, 7, 9.
  b Find the median of 5, 4, 8, 7, 1, 3, 4, 6.

2 Copy and complete
  a The mean of 3, 5, 7 and ☐ is 5.
  b The mean of 4, 6, 7, 8 and ☐ is 7.

3 For this set of numbers: 4, 0, 6, −2, 4, 7, 4 and 9 find
  a the mean
  b the median
  c the range
  d the mode.

4 The frequency table shows the heights of 40 plants.

Height h, cm	Frequency
$0 < h \leqslant 10$	11
$10 < h \leqslant 20$	13
$20 < h \leqslant 30$	10
$30 < h \leqslant 40$	6

  a Write the class interval that contains the median.
  b Work out an estimate for the mean height of the plants.
  c Explain why your answer is an **estimate** of the mean height.

5 An old lady has 8 cats and 10 dogs.
  The mean weight of the cats is 4·5 kg.
  The mean weight of the dogs is 9·2 kg.
  a Calculate the mean weight of all 18 pets.
  b The mean weight of the old lady and her pets is 9·4 kg.
  Calculate the weight of the old lady.

6 The table shows the three-monthly profits, in thousands of pounds, of a sports shop.

	Jan–March	April–June	July–Aug	Sept–Dec
2005	14	22	16	28
2006	13	25	16	31

  a Calculate the 3-point moving averages.
  b Plot these values on a graph.
  c Comment on the trend in the shop's profits over the period.

Homework 8B ⓒ

8.2 pages 391–399

1 The pie chart shows where 180 families spent their holidays. How many families spent their holidays in Spain?

2 There are 500 people working for a company. As part of a health and fitness campaign 25 of the people are weighed. The results are shown in the table.

Weight (*w* kg)	Frequency
$40 < w \leqslant 50$	3
$50 < w \leqslant 60$	8
$60 < w \leqslant 70$	7
$70 < w \leqslant 80$	5
$80 \leqslant w \leqslant 90$	2

Estimate the number of people working for the company whose weight is between 60 kg and 70 kg.

3 A company sells its perfume on four continents.
In one particular year
40% was sold in Europe
35% was sold in North America
15% was sold in Asia
10% was sold in Africa
a What angles would you draw on a pie chart to represent this information?
b In the following year the angle representing sales in Africa was 45°.
What percentage of sales was in Africa that year?

4 Here is a stem-and-leaf diagram showing the heights of the children in a playgroup.
a How many children were in the playgroup?
b What was the range of the heights?
c Find the median height.

Stem	Leaf
8	0 3 4 5
9	0 1 1 5 6 9
10	1 2 3 7 8
11	5 5

Key 11|5 means 115 cm

5 Here are the marks of 27 children in a spelling test.

33   40   62   56   73   87   53   81   44
57   75   34   82   86   42   94   62   37
45   80   64   75   38   67   58   90   46

a Draw a stem-and-leaf diagram.
b Find the median mark in the test.

Homework 8C⊙

8.3 pages 400–414

1 Describe the correlation, if any, in each of these scatter graphs.

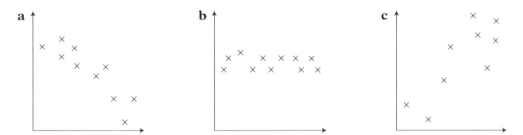

2 The table gives details of the area of farmland and its selling price.

Area, hectares	4	13	7	8	13	16	13	5
Price, £	5000	11 000	8000	10 000	14 000	15 000	12 000	7000

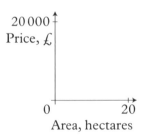

a Plot the points on a scatter diagram and draw a line of best fit.
b Estimate the selling price of Oaklands Farm which has an area of 17·5 hectares.

3 Sam is planning to open a shop selling coffee, tea and snacks.
He writes a questionnaire to find out what sort of drinks and snacks people want.
a Write a suitable question that would help him to find the information he is looking for.
b He asks his grandfather 'would you prefer tea or coffee in the shop?'
Give two reasons to explain why this is not a reliable way to find the sort of information he is looking for.

4 The table shows information about 200 passengers on an aircraft.

Age (A years)	Number of male passengers	Number of female passengers
$0 < A \leqslant 10$	5	10
$10 < A \leqslant 20$	30	20
$20 < A \leqslant 30$	20	40
$30 < A \leqslant 40$	15	35
$40 < A \leqslant 50$	10	15

One of the stewards on the plane wants to conduct a survey to find out why the passengers chose that airline. He takes a sample, stratified both by age and gender, of 20 of the passengers.

a Calculate the number of males aged 10–20 he should sample.
b Calculate the number of females aged 20–40 he should sample.

Homework 8D ⓒ

8.7 pages 420–427

1 The cumulative frequency diagram shows the weights of 80 people in a school.
Use the diagram to estimate
a the median weight
b the interquartile range.
c The smallest weight was 18 kg and the greatest weight was 87 kg.
Draw a box plot to show this information.

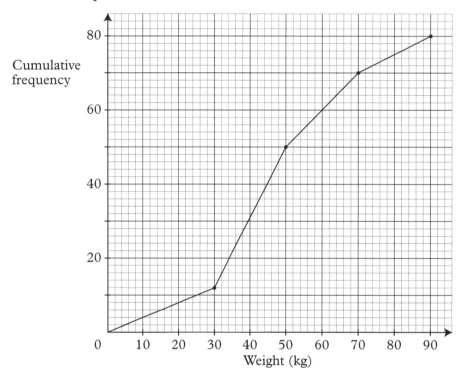

2 Sue and Adam both play darts. The box plots show their
scores with three darts in several games.

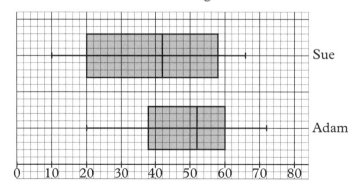

a Write the median and the interquartile range for Sue.
b Write the median and the interquartile range for Adam.
c Which player is more consistent? Give a reason for your answer.
d Who do you think is the better player? Give a reason.

3 As part of a test of a fertiliser, A, a batch of potatoes were weighed.
Copy and complete the table and then draw a cumulative frequency
diagram for the results.

Fertiliser
A

Weight w (gm)	Frequency	Cumulative Frequency
$100 < w \leqslant 200$	0	0 ($\leqslant 200$)
$200 < w \leqslant 300$	14	14 ($\leqslant 300$)
$300 < w \leqslant 400$	30	44
$400 < w \leqslant 500$	28	
$500 < w \leqslant 600$	8	

b Find the median weight of the potatoes.
c Find the interquartile range of the weights of the potatoes.

A second batch of potatoes were grown using fertiliser B.
The weights of the potatoes are shown in the box plot.

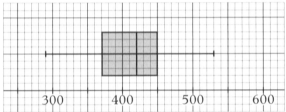 with fertiliser B

d Write the median and the interquartile range for fertiliser B.
e Describe the difference in the results for the two fertilisers.

Homework 8E

8.8 pages 428–432

1 The histogram shows information
about the weights of pieces of
model furniture.
a How many of the weights
are in these intervals
i 10–20 g   **ii** 20–25 g?
b How many pieces were
there altogether?

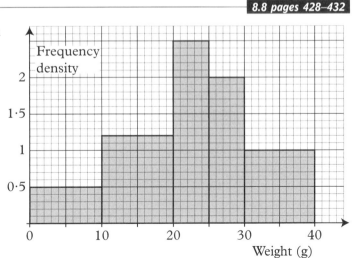

2 The table shows the ages of the people at a hotel in a skiing region.

Age, x (years)	Frequency
$0 < x \leqslant 10$	18
$10 < x \leqslant 20$	26
$20 < x \leqslant 25$	30
$25 < x \leqslant 35$	22
$35 < x \leqslant 50$	30

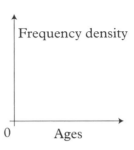

Draw a histogram to illustrate these data.

3 This histogram shows the heights, in metres, of the trees in a wood.
There were 20 trees in the class 0–10 m.

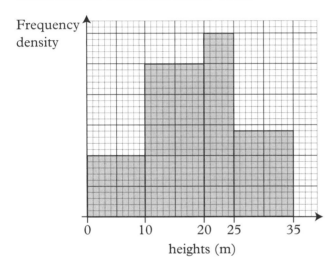

Work out the numbers on the frequency density axis and hence find the total number of trees in the wood.

4 This histogram shows the ages of the animals in a zoo.
  a How many animals are aged from 10 to 20 years?
  b How many animals are in the zoo altogether?

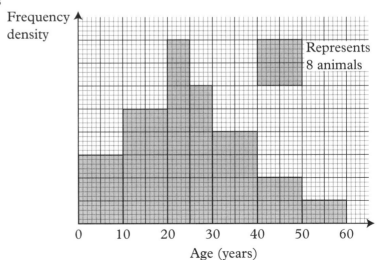

9   Probability

Homework 9A

9.2 pages 442–446

1 Zoë puts cards numbered 2, 3, 4, 5, 6, 7, 8, 9, 10, 11, 12 and 13 in a box. She selects one card at random. Find the probability of that Zoë selects

  a a 10   **b** an odd number
  c a prime number   **d** a square number
  e a number greater than 7   **f** a number less than 15.

2 Tim puts cards lettered A, B, C, D, E, F, G, H, I, J and K in a box. He selects one card at random. Find the probability that Tim selects

  a a D   **b** an I or a J
  c a vowel   **d** a consonant.

3 Adam writes each letter of the word 'PARALLEL' on a card and the 8 cards are placed in a box. Find the probability of selecting

  a an A   **b** a P
  c an L   **d** an R or an E.

4 Eve selects one card at random from the nine cards shown.

Find the probability that Eve selects
  a the ace of diamonds   **b** a king
  c the 8 of spades   **d** a red card.

5 A fair dice is rolled 60 times. How many times would you expect to roll
  a a 1
  b an even number?

6 This spinner is spun 40 times. How many times would you expect to spin
  a an 8
  b a number less than three?

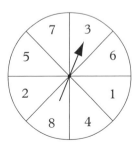

7 Rana puts some balls numbered 1, 2, 3, 4, ..., 30 in a bag.
She selects one ball at random. Find the probability that
Rana selects

  a a 5   **b** a multiple of 5
  c a number less than 10   **d** a prime number
  e a square number   **f** a number greater than 40.

8 Rob puts these numbered balls in a bag.
  a Find the probability of selecting a
       ball numbered 4.
  b Rob puts more balls into the bag so that
       the chance of getting a 5 is **twice** the
       chance of getting a 2. What balls could he
       put in the bag?

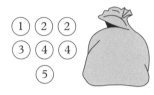

9 A coin is biased so that the chance of getting 'heads' is
twice the chance of getting 'tails'. What is the probability
of getting 'tails'?

10 Here are two bags containing balls. From which bag is
the probability of selecting a white ball greater? You may
use a calculator.

  4 white   7 white
  7 black   13 black

Homework 9B ⓒ

9.2 pages 448–452

1 Emma tosses a 10p coin and a 20p coin at
the same time. Make a list of all the possible
ways in which the coins could land.

2 Harry throws a coin and a dice. He could get a 'head'
and a 2 (H, 2).
Make a list of the 12 possible outcomes.

3 Jack tosses three coins (10p, 20p, 50p) together.
  a Make a list of all the possible out comes.
  b What is the probability that Jack gets three 'tails'?

4 You can choose from 4 possible drinks.

| tea | coffee | orange | water |

I buy a drink for myself and one for my brother. Make a list of all the possible pairs of drinks I could get. What is the probability that I get two coffees?

5 Lucy spins two spinners and adds the numbers. If she gets a 2 and a 6 the total is 8.

  a Copy and complete the table to show all the possible outcomes and totals.

  b Find the probability that Lucy gets a total of 6.

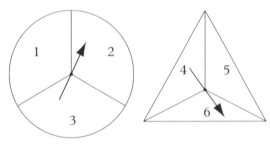

+	4	5	6
1			
2			8
3			

6 Martin rolls a red dice and a white dice and adds the scores.
  a Copy and complete this table to show all the outcomes.
  b Find the probability that Martin gets a total of 4.
  c Find the probability of that Martin gets a total of 6.

+	1	2	3	4	5	6
1						
2			5			
3						9
4						
5						
6						

7 Susie rolls a red dice and a white dice and works out the **difference** between the scores.
  a Make a table similar to the one in question **6** and write the differences.
  b Find the probability that Susie gets a difference of 3.
  c Find the probability that Susie gets a difference which is less than 2.

Homework 9C ⊙

9.3 pages 454–458

1 A coin is biased so that the probability of tossing a 'head' is 0·45.
What is the probability of tossing a 'tail'?

2 A box contains 12 balls: 3 red, 2 yellow, 4 green and
3 white. Find the probability of selecting
  a a red ball   **b** a ball which is **not** red
  c a yellow ball   **d** a ball which is **not** yellow.

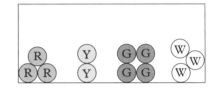

3 A fair dice is rolled. What is the probability of rolling either
a 2 or a 3?

4 A bag contains balls which are either red, white or blue.
The probability of selecting a red ball is 0·3.
The probability of selecting a white ball is 0·35.

  a Find the probability of selecting a blue ball.
  b Find the probability of selecting a ball which is **not** blue.

5 The table shows the probabilities of four people winning
in their next game of golf.

Jane	Susy	Samithra	Deepa
0·3	0·25	x	0·15

  a What is the probability that either Susy or Deepa wins?
  b What is the probability that Samithra wins?
  c What is the probability that Jane does **not** win?

6 The probabilities of a biased dice landing on different
numbers is given in the table.

Number	1	2	3	4	5	6
Probability	0·1	0·15	0·2	0·15	0·3	0·1

  a Herman rolls the dice 300 times. Find an estimate for
the number of times he will roll a 2.
  b Shami rolls the dice once. Find the probability that she
will roll either a 4 or a 5.

7 A student is selected at random from a school. The table shows the
probabilities that the student can or cannot swim.

	Boys	Girls
Can swim	0·32	0·3
Cannot swim	0·2	0·18

  a What is the probability that the student can swim?
  b There are 36 boys in the school who cannot swim. Find the total
number of students in the school.

Homework 9D⒠

9.4 pages 458–460

1 Arthur rolls a fair dice and draws a card from a pack of playing cards.
Find the probability that Arthur
a rolls a 6 on the dice
b selects a red card
c rolls a six and selects a red card.

2 Annabel rolls a dice and tosses a coin. Find the probability
that Annabel
a tosses a 'tail' on the coin and rolls a 2 on the dice
b tosses a 'head' on the coin and rolls an even number
on the dice.

3 A bag contains 10 balls. 6 are red and 4 are white.
Jake selects a ball is at random and then replaces it.
He selects a second ball. Copy and complete the
tree diagram and use it to find the probability that
Jake gets a red ball both times.

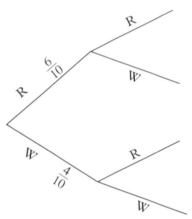

4 A bag contains 7 balls. 5 are green and 2 are white.

Maisie selects a ball and then replaces it. She then selects a
second ball. Draw a tree diagram similar to the one in
question **3**. Find the probability that Maisie selects two balls
of the same colour.

5 The probability that Steve will pass his driving test is 0·3.
The probability that Tina will pass her driving test is 0·4.
The probability that both Steve and Tina will pass their
driving tests is 0·5.
Decide whether or not the events 'Steve will pass his driving test' and
'Tina will pass her driving test' are independent.

6 Wayne throws a fair dice twice.
a Copy and complete the tree diagram.
b Find the probability that Wayne only gets one 2.

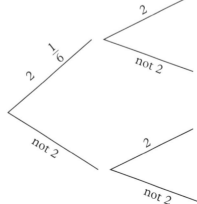

Homework 9E Ⓔ

9.4 pages 462–468

1 A bag contains 6 red balls and 3 black balls.
Tammy selects a ball at random and
does **not** replace it. She then selects a
second ball.
  a Copy and complete the tree diagram.
  b Find the probability that Tammy selects
    i two red balls
    ii a red ball and a black ball (in any order).

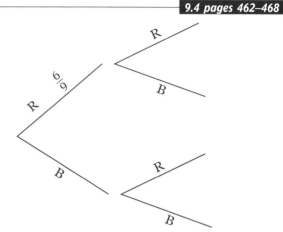

2 Dave throws a fair dice twice. Copy and
complete the tree diagram and show at
each branch the two events '4' and 'not 4'.
Find the probability that Dave throws a total of
  a two 4s   **b** no 4s   **c** one 4.

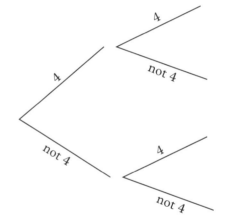

3 Ian has 7 chocolates in a box and they all look the same. Three
chocolates are fruit flavoured and the others are caramel flavoured.
Ian selects one chocolate and eats it. He then selects a second
chocolate.
  a Copy and complete the tree diagram.
  b Find the probability that Ian selects two
    caramel flavoured chocolates.

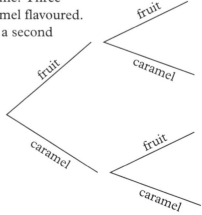

4 Bag A contains 3 red and 2 white balls.
   Bag B contains 4 red and 1 white ball.

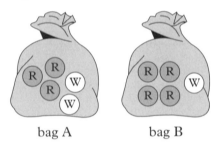

   bag A   bag B

Lincoln selects a ball from bag A and puts it in bag B.
Abraham then selects a ball from bag B.
a Copy and complete the tree diagram.

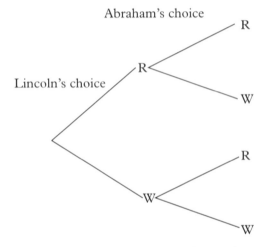

b Find the probability that Abraham selects a white ball.

5 A bag contains n green balls and 5 purple balls.
   Simon selects a ball and does not replace it. He then selects
   a second ball.
   a Find the probability, in terms of n, that Simon will select
      a green ball on both occasions.
   b Given that the answer to part **a** is $\frac{14}{39}$, Find the value of n.

10 Revision

Homework 10A❸ Mixed questions

1 Write the value of $\cos x$.

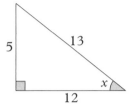

2 Work out, without a calculator
$$\frac{2}{3} - \frac{2}{5}$$

3 Write two hundred million in standard form.

4 The line $y = 3x - 1$ cuts the x-axis at P. Find the coordinates of P.

5 Answer 'true' or 'false' : $29\cdot555 = 30$ correct to two significant figures.

6 Factorise
$$8y^2 + 28y$$

7 Make x the subject of the formula.
$$a(x + b) = m$$

8 Solve this equation.
$$5^x = 1$$

9 Calculate the length of the diagonal of a rectangle measuring 9 cm by 5 cm. Leave your answer in surd form.

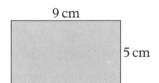

10 Find the nth term in the sequence 2, 5, 8, 11, ...

11 Work out $1530 \div 34$, without a calculator.

12 Factorise
$$x^2 - 7x + 12$$

13 Calculate the average speed of a train which travels 74 km in 30 minutes.

14 How many square tiles of side 50 cm will Bill need to cover this floor?

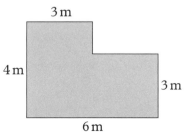

Micah
Lynn

Maths revision

1.

2. $\dfrac{2}{3} - \dfrac{2}{5} = \dfrac{10}{15} - \dfrac{6}{15} = \dfrac{4}{15}$

3. 2×10^8

4. $(0, -1)$

5. True

6.

7. $ax + ab = m$
   $ax = m - ab$
   $x = \dfrac{m - ab}{a}$

8. $x = 0.2$

9.

10. $n + 3$

11.

13. 148 mph

14. 84

15. $\cancel{8}$ 2,3,3,5, 7, 8, 11, 13, 13) 7?

16)

17)

$2x + 1$

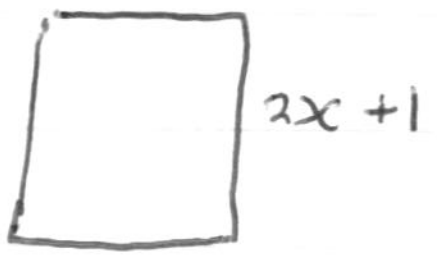

15 Find the median of
5, 8, 2, 11, 13, 3, 7 and 13.

16 Solve this equation.
$9n^2 = 16$

17 The perimeter of this rectangle is 40 cm.
Find x.

$17 - x$

$2(x + 1)$

Homework 10B C

1 Given that $a = \frac{5}{8}$, $b = \frac{3}{4}$ and $c = \frac{5}{7}$, which of these statements
is true?

   A $a > b > c$ B $b > c > a$ C $c > b > a$

2 Find x, if $9^x = 27$.

3 Find the approximate value of
$$\frac{71 \cdot 7 \times 106}{33 \cdot 8}$$
Show your working.

4 Work out the area of the trapezium.

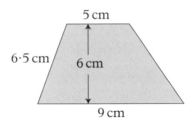

5 cm

6·5 cm

6 cm

9 cm

5 Find x and y if
$xy = 60$ and $x - y = 4$.

6 Find the gradient of the line $3x + y = 6$.

7 ABCD is a cyclic quadrilateral.
Find the size of angle DBC.

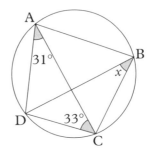

A

$31°$

B

x

D

$33°$

C

8 Find the value of x which satisfies these simultaneous equations.

$$4x - y = 7$$
$$x + y = 3$$

9 Work out, without a calculator, $-7 + (-7)$.

10 Convert $\frac{5}{9}$ to a recurring decimal.

11 ABCD is a rectangle with
AB = 9 cm, BC = 7 cm, CX = 3 cm
and YC = 4 cm.
Find the shaded area.

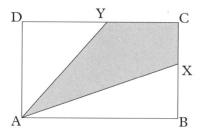

12 Work out 6% of a quarter of £212.

Homework 10C 🟢

1 Five people each toss a coin. What is the probability that the fifth person will toss a 'head'?

2 Find the value of $0.9 - 0.75$ as a fraction.

3 Given that $n^3 = 200$, find the value of n correct to the nearest whole number.

4 Calculate the length of the side marked x.

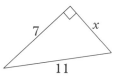

5 A computer is bought for £250 and sold for £330. Calculate the profit as a percentage of the original price.

6 Simplify

$$(x + 2)(x - 1) - 2(x + 1)$$

7 The curve with equation $y = (x + 2)(x - 3)$ cuts the axes at A, B and C. What are the coordinates of A, B and C?

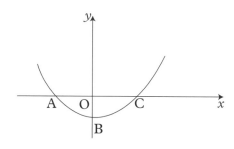

8 A bag contains 3 red balls, 5 blue balls and 8 yellow balls. One ball is selected at random. Find the probability of selecting a blue ball.

9 Solve this equation.

$$\frac{8}{x-1} = 4$$

10 Find the size of the angle marked p.

11 Estimate, correct to one significant figure

$$\sqrt{104\cdot7} \times 29\,715$$

12 Find the values of x which satisfy the inequality

$$3x + 1 > 3 - 2x$$

13 Given that $a = 3$ and $b = -4$, what is the value of ab^2?

14 The point P(7, 2) is reflected in the line $y = x$.
Write the coordinates of the image of P.

Homework 10D ⓒ

1 Given $a = 4$, $b = -3$, $c = 2$, work out the values of these expressions.
  a abc **b** $c^2 - b^2$ **c** $a - b$

2 Write the prime numbers between 15 and 30.

3 Which of the following is/are correct?

  A $3^2 = 81^{\frac{1}{2}}$ B $4 \div 0\cdot1 = 40$ C $(-5)^0 < 0$

4 Find the length x.
All lengths are in cm.

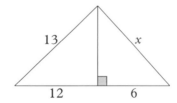

5 Kelly invested £2000 at 4% compound interest.
How much was her investment worth after 3 years?

6 a Express $x^2 - 6x - 3$ in the form $(x - a)^2 - b$
    where a and b are positive integers.
  b Hence write the minimum value of $x^2 - 6x - 3$.

7 Find n if $(a^5)^3 \div a^6 = a^n$.

8 The total surface area of a cube is 96 cm². Find the volume of the cube.

9 Sketch the graph of $y = 2^x$ for positive and negative values of x.

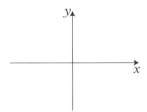

10 Simplify

$$\frac{(3x)^2 - 6x}{12xy^2}.$$

11 A fair dice is rolled five times and shows a 6 each time. What is the probability that it will show a 6 on the next roll?

12 The area of the square is 4 cm² greater than the area of the rectangle. Form an equation and solve it to find x.

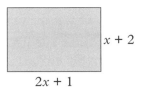

$x + 2$

$2x + 1$

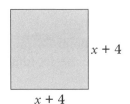

$x + 4$

$x + 4$

13 Mark tossed a fair coin and a fair dice. What is the probability that Mark gets a head and a 6?

14 Solve this equation.

$$\frac{1}{x} + \frac{3}{x + 1} = 4$$

Homework 10E 🅲

1 Factorise $2n^2 + 7n - 4$.

2 Solve these simultaneous equations.

$2x - y = 8$
$3x + 2y = 5$

3 Find the shaded area in this square. Leave π in your answer.

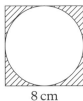

8 cm

4 After a pay rise of 3% Mr Atkins earned £18 952 per year. How much did he earn before the increase?

5 Write down the nth term of this sequence.

$$\frac{2}{4}, \frac{3}{5}, \frac{4}{6}, \frac{5}{7}, \ldots$$

6 Which of the following is/are correct?

A $\frac{2}{3} \div \frac{7}{9} = \frac{6}{7}$　　　　B $10^6\,\text{mm} = 1\,\text{km}$　　　　C $0{\cdot}6^2 > 0{\cdot}6$

7 A cube has a volume of $300\,\text{cm}^3$. Find the length of each side of the cube. Give your answer correct to 2 decimal places.

8 Find the length x.

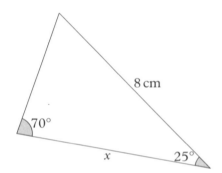

9 A shop offers '30% off' in its sale. A coat cost £52·50 in the sale. Calculate the original price of the coat.

10 The heights of 200 plants were measured.
The results are in the table.
Calculate the mean height of the plants.

Height	Frequency
8 cm	30
9 cm	70
10 cm	80
11 cm	20

11 At what point does the line $y = x + 5$ meet the line $y = 3x - 1$?

12 Work out, without a calculator

$$(3{\cdot}2 \times 10^{14}) \times (2 \times 10^{-5})$$

13 Make x the subject of this formula.

$$x + a = \frac{x}{b}$$

14 Sketch a scatter graph showing strong negative correlation.

Homework 10F

1 Calculate the perimeter of the semicircle.
   Take $\pi = \frac{22}{7}$.

2 $y = \frac{ab}{a+b}$, $a = 4 \times 10^5$, $b = 3 \times 10^4$.
   Find y, giving your answer in standard form.

3 Solve the inequality $6 - x^2 < 5$.

4 Make w the subject of this formula.
   $$p = \frac{10 + 2w}{12}$$

5 Answer 'true' or 'false'.
   $$7n^0 > (7n)^0$$

6 Work out $\sin x + \tan x$.

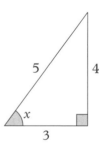

7 Convert $6\,\text{m}^3$ into cm^3.

8 Sketch the curve $y = 8 - x^2$.

9 Solve these simultaneous equations.
   $$x + 2y = 4$$
   $$5x - 6y = 28$$

10 Factorise $6x^2 + x - 2$.

11 $\overrightarrow{OA} = \mathbf{a}$, $\overrightarrow{OB} = \mathbf{b}$, M is the midpoint of AB.
   Express $\overrightarrow{OM}$ in terms of $\mathbf{a}$ and $\mathbf{b}$.

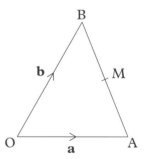

12 A solid sphere has a volume of $100\,\text{cm}^3$.
   Calculate the radius of the sphere. ($V = \frac{4}{3}\pi r^3$)

13 Solve the equation
   $$2x = \frac{3}{x} - 5$$

14 p is inversely proportional to the square of x.
   When $x = 2$, $p = 12$.
   Calculate the value of x when $p = 1\frac{1}{3}$.

Homework 10G

1 n is an integer such that $-10 \leqslant 3n \leqslant 9$. Find possible values of n.

2 You are given that $\sin 30° = \dfrac{1}{2}$, $\cos 30° = \dfrac{\sqrt{3}}{2}$.

   a Find the area of the triangle.

   b Find x.

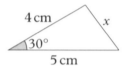

3 Express $x^2 + x + 1$ in the form $(x + a)^2 + b$.

4 Share £441 in the ratio $2 : 7$.

5 The table shows the marks obtained by 10 students in a test.

Mark	2	3	4
Frequency	5	3	2

  Calculate the mean mark in the test.

6 $n = 3^x$, $m = 3^y$

  Express in terms of n and/or m.

  a 3^{x+y}

  b 3^{y-1}

7 Solve the equation

$$\frac{4}{x + 1} = \frac{2}{3}$$

8 Make T the subject of the formula

$$\frac{2x + 1}{10} = \frac{T}{T + 5}$$

9 Here is a list of 5 numbers in order of size.

   ☐   5   ☐   10   ☐

  The mean of the numbers is 5. The median is 6. The range is 12. Find the missing numbers.

10 AB is an arc of a circle of radius 21 cm.
Find the length of arc AB.

   Take $\pi = \dfrac{22}{7}$.

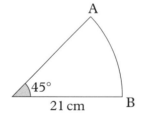

11 Write as a single fraction.

$$\frac{4}{x} - \frac{x}{x + 1}$$

11 Examination style questions

Homework 11A

1 a Express 504 as the product of its prime factors.

  b Work out $4\frac{2}{3} - 2\frac{3}{4}$

2 a Solve this equation.
$$3(2x - 5) - x = 2x + 3$$

  b Rearrange $y = ax + c$ to make x the subject.

3 ABCD is a parallelogram.
Prove that triangle ABD is congruent to triangle CDB.

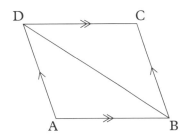

4 Put these numbers in order of size, smallest first.

$5 \cdot 3^2$ $\sqrt{800}$ $11 \cdot 2\%$ of 310

5 Here are the first 5 terms of a sequence.

4   10   16   22   28

Find an expression, in terms of n, for the nth term of the sequence.

6 a Factorise completely.

$3a^2 + 3ab - 3a$

b Factorise.

$x^2 - 2x - 24$

7 The diagram shows the position of three towers A, B and C.
The bearing of C from B is 140°. B is due east of A.
The distance from A to B is equal to the distance from B to C.

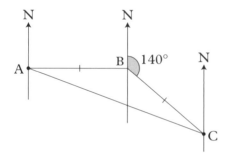

Work out the bearing of A from C.

8 Here are some expressions.

$\pi c \qquad \frac{1}{4}ab^2 \qquad 3(a+b) \qquad \frac{\pi}{3}a^2 \qquad (a+2c)^2 \qquad \frac{ac}{b}$

The letters a, b and c represent lengths.

a Write the three expressions that could represent lengths.

b Write the expression that could represent a volume.

9

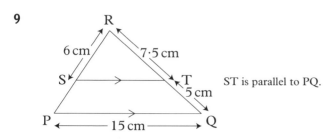

ST is parallel to PQ.

a Calculate the length of SP.

b Calculate the length of ST.

Homework 11B

1 Look at this list of numbers.

2 5 8 9 30 54

From this list, write down

a a square number

b a cube number

c a multiple of 15

d a factor of 27.

2 Simplify fully.

a $3(2x + 1) - 2(x - 2)$

b $(2xy^2)^3$

c $\dfrac{(n - 2)(n + 1)}{(n - 2)} \times \dfrac{2n}{(n + 1)}$

3 Shapes ABCD and EFGH are mathematically similar.

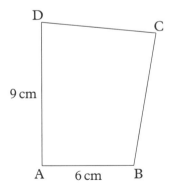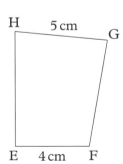

a Calculate the length of EH.

b Calculate the length of DC.

4 Solve these simultaneous equations.

$2x + 3y = 4$

$3x - y = 17$

5 Find an approximate value of

$$\frac{52 \cdot 3 \times 4 \cdot 11}{(9.89)^2}$$

You must show your working.

6 The area of the square is 30 times the area of the triangle.
Work out the length of each side of the square.

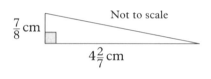

$\frac{7}{8}$ cm

Not to scale

$4\frac{2}{7}$ cm

7 Here are five numbers written in standard form.

$3 \cdot 2 \times 10^3$ $4 \cdot 5 \times 10^{-2}$ $8 \cdot 4 \times 10^7$ $1 \cdot 7 \times 10^4$ $6 \cdot 66 \times 10^6$

a Find the largest number.

b Find the smallest number.

c Write $4 \cdot 5 \times 10^{-2}$ as an ordinary number.

d Work out $(3 \cdot 2 \times 10^3) + (1 \cdot 7 \times 10^4)$.
    Give your answer in standard form.

8 A straight line, L, passes through the point $(5, 17)$ and is parallel to the
line with equation $y = 3x - 12$.
Find the equation of the straight line, L.

9 The rectangle shown has sides of length x cm and $3x$ cm.
The diagonals of the rectangle are each of length 30 cm.

x cm

$3x$ cm

Calculate the area of the rectangle.

10 Point O is the centre of a circle of radius 8 cm.
Angle AOB is 40°.

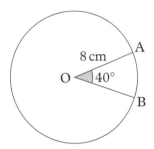

Calculate the area of sector AOB.
Give your answer in terms of π.

Homework 11C

1 Using the information that $63 \times 213 = 13\,419$, write the value of

 a 6.3×213

 b 0.63×213

 c $6.3 \times 21\,300$

2 a Factorise completely.
   $15x^2 - 10x$

 b n is an integer. List the values of n such that
   $-8 \leqslant 4n < 16$

3 Cylinders A and B are mathematically similar.
The lengths of the cylinders are shown on the diagram.
The volume of cylinder B is 96 cm³.
Calculate the volume of cylinder A.

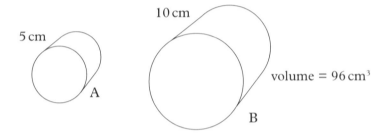

10 cm

5 cm

A

volume = 96 cm³

B

4 Three students used their calculators to work out the value of

$$\frac{32 \cdot 56}{5 \cdot 14 \times 0 \cdot 97}.$$

Their answers, correct to 3 significant figures, were 0·417, 6·53 and 23·7.
Use approximations to decide which one of the answers is correct.
You must show your working.

5 The diagram shows two circles of radii r cm
and R cm.

$r = 2 \cdot 3$ to 1 decimal place
$R = 8 \cdot 9$ to 1 decimal place

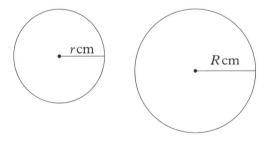

r cm

R cm

a Copy and complete
Upper bound of $r =$
Lower bound of $r =$
Upper bound of $R =$
Lower bound of $R =$

b Find the smallest possible value of $R - r$.

6 a Expand and simplify $(a + b)^2$

   b Hence or otherwise find the value of
$$5{\cdot}04^2 + 2 \times 5{\cdot}04 \times 1{\cdot}96 + 1{\cdot}96^2$$

7 The price of a lawnmower was increased by 10%.
The price after the increase was £401·50.
Calculate the price before the increase.

> Remember:
> Do not use a
> calculator!

8 a i Evaluate $5n^0$

   ii Evaluate $(5n)^0$

   b Work out $7\frac{1}{2} \div \frac{5}{8}$

9 Draw a grid like the one shown.
Indicate clearly the region defined by the three inequalities

$x \geqslant 2$
$y \geqslant x - 2$
$x + y \leqslant 6$

Mark the region with the letter R.

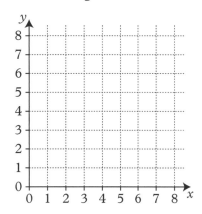

10 Rationalise the denominator of $\dfrac{4 + \sqrt{5}}{\sqrt{5}}$
Simplify your answer fully.

Homework 11D

1 Make x the subject of
$3(x - 2) = y(5 - x)$

2 Solve these simultaneous equations.
$$y = x - 5$$
$$3x + 2y = 0$$

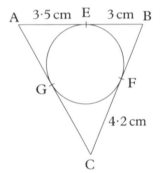

3 The sides of triangle ABC are tangents
to the circle.
AE = 3·5 cm
EB = 3 cm
CF = 4·2 cm
Calculate the perimeter of the triangle ABC.

4 The table shows values of n and y
taken during an experiment.

n	2	4	5
y	12	48	75

Which of these rules fits the results?

a $y \propto n$　　　　　　**b** $y \propto n^2$　　　　　　**c** $y \propto n^3$

You must show your working.

5 The diagram shows a solid metal cylinder of radius 4 cm and height 3 cm.

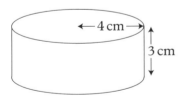

a Find the volume of the cylinder, giving your answer in terms of π.

b The cylinder is melted down and recast as a solid sphere of radius r cm.
Find the value of r.
Give your answer as a surd.

6 a Copy and complete the table for $y = 2x^2 - 3x - 3$.

x	−2	−1	0	1	2	3
y		2				

b i Draw a grid like the one shown.

    ii Draw the graph of $y = 2x^2 - 3x - 3$
       for values of x from -2 to $+3$.

c Use your graph to find two approximate
   solutions to the equation $2x^2 - 3x - 3 = 0$.

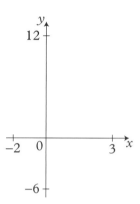

7 In the triangle ABC

   AB = 7 cm
   AC = 8 cm
   Angle BAC = 60°

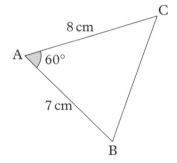

Given that $\cos 60° = \dfrac{1}{2}$, calculate the length of BC.
Give your answer as a surd.

8 a Express $x^2 - 8x + 10$ in the form $(x - a)^2 - b$.

   b Hence solve the equation $x^2 - 8x + 10 = 0$
      Write your answers in the form $x = p \pm \sqrt{q}$.

Homework 11E

1 a Expand and simplify.
$5(2x - 3) - 3(2x + 1)$

b Factorise
$n^2 - n$

c Solve this inequality.
$5x - 3 \leqslant 2x - 12$

2 The cost of a new building is made up of two parts as shown in the table.

Cost of land	£110 000
Cost of building	£1150 per m²

A builder buys the land and builds a house with an area of 192 m².
He later sells the house for £495 000.
Calculate the profit made by the builder.

3 Copy and complete these calculations.

a $-8 + 13 = \square$

b $-2 \times -5 = \square$

c $\square - 5 = -7$

d $-36 \div \square = 9$

4 A straight line has equation $y = \frac{1}{4}x - 3$.

  a The point $(n, 6)$ lies on the straight line.
    Find the value of n.

  b Write the equation of a straight line that is perpendicular to
    $y = \frac{1}{4}x - 3$

5 The price of a dress is reduced by 40% in the sales.
  The sale price is £80·70.
  Calculate the original price of the dress.

6 a Calculate the volume of the cylinder shown in the diagram.

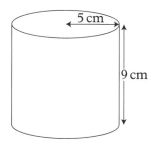

5 cm

9 cm

  The cylinder is solid.
  b Calculate the total surface area of the cylinder.

7 Convert the recurring decimal, $0 \cdot \dot{3}\dot{1}$, to a fraction.

8 The diagram shows a circle with centre O and diameter PR.

Angle PRQ = 32° and angle PSQ = 90°.

a Find the size of angle SPQ.

b Find the size of angle POQ.

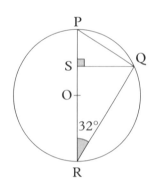

9 This is a sketch of the curve with equation $y = f(x)$.
The vertex of the curve is at $V(-3, -1)$.

a Write the coordinates of the vertex of the curve with equation

   i $y = f(x - 3)$

   ii $y = f(x) + 5$

   iii $y = f(-x)$

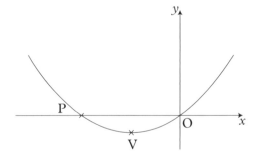

b The curve $y = f(x)$ cuts the x-axis at $O(0, 0)$ and $P(-6, 0)$.

Sketch the curve with equation $y = f\left(\frac{1}{2}x\right)$.

Write the coordinates of the points where this curve meets the x-axis.

Homework 11F

1 Two families share the cost of a holiday house in the ratio $2 : 3$.

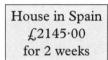

House in Spain
£2145·00
for 2 weeks

Work out the larger share.

2 Calculate the value of $\dfrac{19 \cdot 7 - 12 \cdot 94}{33 \cdot 5 - 19 \cdot 72}$.

  a Write the full calculator display.

  b Give your answer to three significant figures.

3 A van can carry a maximum load of 800 kg, to the nearest 50 kg. It is loaded with packets that weigh 40 kg, to the nearest kg. What is the maximum number of packets it can carry?

4 Louise invests some money in a bank for 15 years at 5% compound interest.
Which graph best shows the value of Louise's investment over the 15 years?

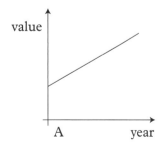
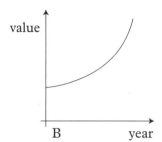
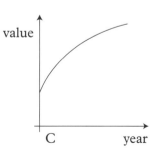

5 The ratio of the surface areas of two similar objects is $1:9$.
What is the ratio of their volumes?

6 Find a. Give your answer in standard form to 2 significant figures.

$$a^2 = \frac{xy}{x-y} \quad \text{and} \quad \begin{aligned} x &= 4{\cdot}1 \times 10^7 \\ y &= 7 \times 10^6 \end{aligned}$$

7 An athlete runs at an average speed of 8 km/h and completes his race in 1 hour 45 minutes. How far does he run?

8 a Which one of these fractions is a recurring decimal?

$$\frac{17}{20} \qquad \frac{7}{8} \qquad \frac{3}{11} \qquad \frac{2}{5}$$

   b Express $\frac{2}{9}$ as a recurring decimal.

   c Find the fraction equivalent to $0{\cdot}3\dot{7}$.

9 The equation $x^3 + x^2 = 400$ has a solution between $x = 7$ and $x = 8$.
Use a trial and improvement method to find the solution.
Give your answer correct to 1 decimal place.

10 Phil bought a yacht for £60 000.
Each year the value of the yacht depreciated by 10%.
Calculate the value of the yacht three years after she bought it.

Homework 11G

1 The diagram shows a semicircle of diameter 13 cm.
Calculate the area of the semicircle.

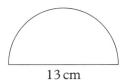

13 cm

Give your answer to three significant figures.

2 a i Solve this inequality.

$4x - 11 < 2x - 3$

ii On a copy of this number line, represent the solution set to part **i**.

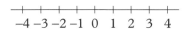
−4 −3 −2 −1 0 1 2 3 4

b Solve this inequality.

$x^2 + 5 \leqslant 9$

3 T and P are both positive quantities.
T is directly proportional to the square root of P.
When T = 10, P = 4.

a Express T in terms of P.

b Find the value of T when P = 100.

c Find the value of P when T = 35.

4 A tank has a rectangular base 40 cm long and
20 cm wide. It contains water to a depth of 10 cm.
Ten spheres of radius 2 cm are placed in the tank.
Calculate how much the water level rises.

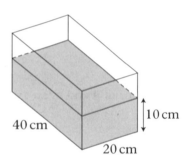

40 cm

20 cm

10 cm

5 Each graph represents one of these equations.

A $y = x^3 + x + 2$

B $y = 3^x$

C $y = 4 - x^2$

P

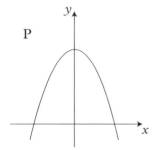

Q

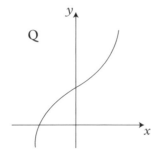

R

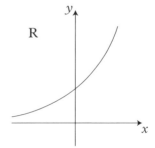

a Write the letter of the equation represented by each graph.

b Write the coordinates of the point where the graph of equation A
meets the *y*-axis.

c Write the coordinates of the point where the graph of equation B
meets the *y*-axis.

6 OAB is a triangle.
N is the point on AB for which BN : NA = 3 : 2.
$\overrightarrow{OA} = \mathbf{a}$ and $\overrightarrow{OB} = \mathbf{b}$

a Write in terms of $\mathbf{a}$ and $\mathbf{b}$, an expression for $\overrightarrow{BA}$.

b Express $\overrightarrow{ON}$ in terms of $\mathbf{a}$ and $\mathbf{b}$.
Simplify your answer as far as possible.

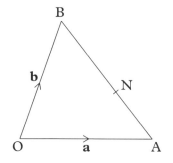

Homework 11H

1 The diagram shows a right-angled triangle ABC.
Work out the length of AB.
Give your answer correct to 3 significant figures.

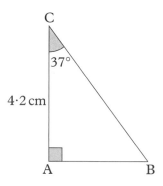

2 a Expand and simplify.
$(x - y)^2$

b Factorise completely.
$12a^2 - 3b^2$

c Rearrange to make e the subject.
$m(t + e) = h$

3 Here are some expressions.

$$\pi a^2 + r^2 \qquad a(b^2 + r^2) \qquad \frac{3a^2b}{r} \qquad 4r + 3a \qquad \pi r^2(a + b)$$

The letters *a*, *b* and *r* represent lengths. π is a number that has no dimensions.
Write the expressions that can represent volumes.

4 The diagram shows a sector of a circle with a radius of 8 cm.

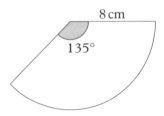

a Work out the area of this sector.

b Work out the arc length of this sector.

c The sector forms the curved surface of a cone.
  Work out the radius, *r* cm, of the base of the cone.

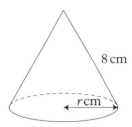

5 The diagram shows a cyclic quadrilateral ABCD.

Angle ADC = 3*x*
Angle ABC = (2*x* + 40°)
Angle DCE = 69°

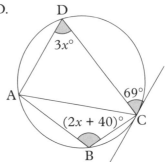

a Work out the value of *x*.

b Find the size of angle DAC.

Give reasons for your answers.

6 In the triangle OPQ

$\overrightarrow{OA}$ = **a**
$\overrightarrow{OB}$ = **b**
OA : AP = 1 : 2
OB : BP = 1 : 3

a Express $\overrightarrow{AQ}$ in terms of **a** and **b**.

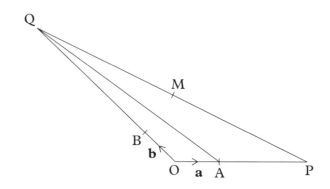

b M is the midpoint of PQ.
Express $\overrightarrow{PM}$ in terms of **a** and **b**.

7 A box contains 10 light bulbs: 3 bulbs are faulty and 7 are not faulty.
Thierry chooses 2 bulbs at random from the box.

a Copy and complete the tree
diagram showing how the
light bulbs could be
chosen.

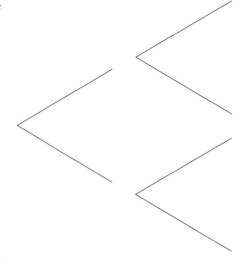

b What is the probability that
Thierry chooses two bulbs
that are faulty?

Homework 11I

1 The force, F, between two bodies is inversely proportional to the square of the distance, x, between them.
When $x = 2$, $F = 24$.

 a Find an expression for F in terms of x.

 b Calculate F when $x = 10$.

2 a Draw a grid like the one shown.

 b Here are four inequalities.

 $3x + 2y < 12$ $y < x$ $y > 0$ $x > 0$

 On the grid, mark with a cross each
 of the points which satisfy all four
 inequalities.

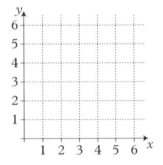

 c Write the coordinates of the points you found.

3 The diagram shows two circles with centre O.
$R = 7{\cdot}7$ correct to 1 decimal place.
$r = 5{\cdot}8$ correct to 1 decimal place.

 a What is the maximum possible diameter
 of the outer circle?

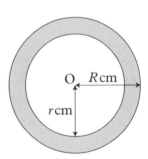

 b Work out the maximum possible area of the
 shaded region. Give your answer correct to five
 significant figures.

4 Solve these simultaneous equations.
$$x^2 + y^2 = 25$$
$$4x - 3y = 0$$

5 a Make k the subject of this formula.
$$\sqrt{k} - m = u^2$$

  b Make y the subject of this formula.
$$m = \pi y + 3y - 4t$$

6 In the diagram, PR is a tangent to the circle with centre at O.
Angle BQR = 61°

  a Calculate the size of angle BQA.

  b Calculate the size of angle BAQ.
  Give reasons for your answers.

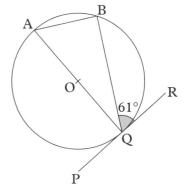

7 a Solve $4(2x + 1) - 3x = 2(3 - x)$.

  b Factorise fully.
$$x^2 + 7x + 6$$

  c Simplify as far as possible.
$$\frac{(x - 2)}{(x^2 + 7x + 6)} \times \frac{(x^2 - 1)}{(2x - 4)}$$

8 AB = 8·2 m
BC = 11·9 m
Angle ABC = 48°

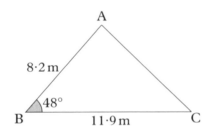

a Calculate the area of triangle ABC.
Give your answer correct to 3 significant figures.

b Calculate the length of AC.
Give your answer to 3 significant figures.